HAIDER

Vishal Bhardwaj is a critically acclaimed Hindi film director, writer, screenwriter, producer, music composer and playback singer. Born in Bijnore and raised in Meerut in Uttar Pradesh, Bhardwaj studied at Hindu College, University of Delhi. Known for his collaboration with filmmaker and lyricist Gulzar – he shot into fame when he scored the music for Gulzar's *Maachis* – Bhardwaj has directed such films as *Kaminey, 7 Khoon Maaf* and *Matru ki Bijli ka Mandola*. *Haider*, adapted from *Hamlet*, is part of a trilogy of films based on Shakespeare's plays directed by Bhardwaj, the other two being *Maqbool* (adapted from *Macbeth*) and *Omkara* (adapted from *Othello*).

HAIDER

The Original Screenplay
(with English translation)

Vishal Bhardwaj
with Basharat Peer

HarperCollins *Publishers* India

First published in hardback in 1997
by HarperCollins *Publishers* India in

HarperCollins Publishers India, Cyber City, Building 10-A, Gurugram,
Haryana-122002, India
www.harpercollins.co.in

2 4 6 8 10 9 7 5 3

P-ISBN: 978-93-5136-987-5
E-ISBN: 978-93-5136-988-2

Typeset in Sabon 11.5/14 and Shiva 12.5/14.5
by Ram Das Lal, New Delhi (NCR)

Printed and bound at
MicroPrints India, New Delhi

MIX
Paper
FSC FSC® C218906

This product is made of FSC®-certified and other controlled material.

HarperCollins Publishers, Macken House, 39/40 Mayor Street
Upper, Dublin 1, D01 C9W8, Ireland

Preface

After *Omkara* I wanted a break from Shakespeare. I wanted to explore some original story ideas. I also wanted the feeling that I must complete my trilogy of Shakespeare's tragedies hanging over me, so that there was always something to go back to. After every film I used to think of *King Lear* and *Hamlet,* in that order. I had a great setting for *King Lear* but it was the sexual conflict of *Hamlet* that made me decide in its favour. Since both my previous tragedies had the man-woman relationship at their core, I thought *Hamlet* would be the best story to complete the trilogy. I would have waited a few more years to make it but a few of my fellow filmmakers announced adaptations of *Hamlet* and that actually pushed me to speed up to reach home before them.

My dear writer friend from Mussoorie, Steve Alter, had this great idea to adapt *Hamlet* into an espionage thriller. I also personally feel that we haven't made a good espionage film as yet. Our external intelligence service, RAW, is so secretive of its operations – failures and successes both – and so invisible that unlike in the West, we hardly get to see or read about their work. Thus whatever we project in films becomes unreal and fictitious.

Steve worked out a beautiful plot where Claudius implicates Horwendil, who works in RAW, into a mole of a foreign intelligence service. Horwendil has to take asylum in a foreign country and thus has to live with a 'ghost' identity. I found this ghost angle to be very fascinating and exciting. We interacted further and Steve worked out a complete structure of our espionage *Hamlet*.

I always go to Gulzar Saab for the final approval and he was the one who pointed out that it was no doubt a good thriller but where was the tragedy in it? I suddenly realized that the genre had changed from a tragedy to a thriller. I was depressed again.

One night I woke up to find my wife Rekha crying while reading a book titled *Curfewed Nights* by Basharat Peer. She explained that it was a memoir of the writer's growing-up years in the nineties – the peak period of militancy in the Kashmir valley. A bulb switched on in my head. I strongly feel that Kashmir has been the biggest tragedy of modern Indian history and no film has been made to capture the real tragedy of what has been going on there for the last twenty-five years. I began to read Basharat's book with *Hamlet* in mind and by the time I finished it I had decided to collaborate with him to work out my version of *Hamlet.*

It turned out to be a very unique experience to work with him on the screenplay of *Haider*. Basharat had two qualities which added a lot to the screenplay – one, since he is a serious journalist, he has so many real-life stories to share from all over the world, and second he was a *Kashmiri.* I wanted to explore the culture of Kashmir and translate that into the celluloid. It was so difficult for me as for the first time I was entering a world I had never seen or experienced. I did not want to write or direct through imagination so I held Basharat's hand and walked back in time with him to feel the pain, terror and tragedy of that time in Kashmir.

Shahid Kapoor was pre-decided for the part as I think he is the finest actor of his age group. That Shraddha Kapoor and Kay Kay Menon would fit so well into their characters as Kashmiris, I honestly had not imagined. It was so hard to convince Tabu to play mother to Shahid. She was reluctant and I could understand her point of view because Bollywood jumps up at the opportunity to brand people. If you play mother once you will only be offered a mother's role for the rest of your life. I wanted Tabu to see that Ghazala is not just an ordinary Indian mother but also one of the most complicated characters of Shakespeare. Any actress would give her right hand to be Gertrude. I am so glad that finally she could see it and agreed to play the part.

Two people without whom this film would not been possible are Madhu Mantena and Siddharth Roy Kapur. Madhu for pushing me to place it in Kashmir, and Siddharth for believing and backing my vision all the way through.

It was a grilling fifty-five days' experience divided between two seasons, autumn and winter. However much you hear about the beauty and suffering of Kashmir, you can't imagine the impact it has over you till you go there. The beauty is blinding, surprising you at every turn, but the suffering is silent, lurking in the air, piercing your soul feebly.

9 September 2014

Vishal Bhardwaj
Mumbai

UTV
UTV MOTION PICTURES IN ASSOCIATION WITH
VISHAL BHARDWAJ PICTURES PRESENTS
A VISHAL BHARDWAJ FILM
Haider
AN ADAPTATION OF
WILLIAM SHAKESPEARE'S "HAMLET"
TABU, SHAHID KAPOOR, SHRADDHA KAPOOR & KAY KAY MENON
PRODUCED BY SIDDHARTH ROY KAPUR, VISHAL BHARDWAJ

FADE IN:

It is the mid-1990s and the insurgency in Kashmir is at its peak. The Indian defence establishment is finding it difficult to penetrate the extremist groups, which are supported by Pakistan and protected by locals. To meet this challenge, the Indian intelligence has formed the 'Ikhwaan-ul-Muslameen', a counter-insurgent militia comprising of surrendered and captured militants. The Ikhwaanis play a key role in reducing militancy in the valley. The Indian government has decided to hold elections within the next six months to show the world that things are under control in Kashmir.

FADE OUT.

1 INT. IB HEADQUARTERS - SRINAGAR - DAY

On a lonely road, two pairs of eyes and a couple of barrels of AK 47s peep through the holes of a barbed bunker outside an unobtrusive building in a posh area of Srinagar.

SUPER:

'INTELLIGENCE BUREAU HEADQUARTERS, GUPKAR ROAD, SRINAGAR'

INSIDE:

A conference room. BRIGADIER MURTHY addresses a handful of senior army and J&K police officers.

BRIGADIER MURTHY
Gentlemen, Delhi has approved Operation Bulbul.
Counter insurgency force बनाने के लिए
हमें जो भी चाहिए... फंड्स, आर्म्स,
इन्टेलिजेंस... सब मिलेगा.
Gentlemen, Delhi has approved Operation Bulbul.
We have complete support to arm, fund and run...
the counterinsurgency force... Complete support!

The table is full of smiles.

BRIGADIER MURTHY
दुशमन का दुशमन हमारा दोस्त है. इसलिए कोई भी ग्रूप या
individual, surrendered militants, detainees,
undertrials, कोई भी... जो हिज़्बुल मुजाहिदीन या पाकिस्तान के
इस प्रॉक्सी वार के खिलाफ हैं, हमारी ऑर्गेनाइज़ेशन
का हिस्सा बन सकते हैं. The organization will
be called 'Ikh...waan...ul'.
The enemy's foes are our friends... Any individual
or group... anyone against the proxy war by
the Hizbul Mujahideen and Pakistan... be they
surrendered militants, detainees or undertrials...
will be our primary recruits. The organization will
be called 'Ikhwaan-ul'...

A senior cop, the Director General Kashmir Police, prompts Murthy to pronounce it correctly.

DGP KASHMIR

इखवाँ-उल-मुसलमीन.

Ikhwaan-ul-Musalmeen.

Murthy looks at DGP and smiles.

BRIGADIER MURTHY

The army will run the operation but your support will be crucial in recruitment and intelligence.

DGP KASHMIR

My boys are with you, Brigadier!

We see DGP turn to ACP PERVEZ LONE. He smiles a deferential, smug smile.

BRIGADIER MURTHY

Let the Bulbul start singing. It's catch and kill.

CUT TO:

2 EXT. ANANTNAG DISTRICT COURT, LAWYER'S CHAMBER - DAY

A man modestly dressed in a suit and wearing an English hat looks silently out of his window. This is KHURRAM MEER, a handsome lawyer in his late forties. An old man behind him waits for him to speak.

KHURRAM

पाकिस्तान ट्रेन्ड था या लोकल ट्रेन्ड?

Was he trained in Pakistan or locally?...

OLD MAN

अनट्रेन्ड था जनाब मिल्टन नहीं था, एक मिल्टन के पीछे-पीछे चलता था, एक मिल्टन ने पिस्टल दिया था छुपा के रखने को, फिर उस मिल्टन ने सरेंडर किया और फौज ले के घर आ गया...

He was untrained, he just idolized a militant. One militant gave him a weapon to hide... the same guy surrendered and informed the army of the weapon.

Khurram turns and looks at him.

KHURRAM

कशमीर में, ऊपर खुदा है और नीचे फौज... समझे...
और फौज का जंतर Armed Forces Special Powers Act...
अफ़स्पा...

In Kashmir, God in the heaven... and the army rules the earth... And the army has its bible... AFSPA (The Armed Forces Special Powers Act).

OLD MAN

खुर्रम साहेब, मेरा बेटा बेकसूर है...
शीराज़ सिनेमा कैम्प में रखा है आर्मी ने...

Khurram saheb, my son is innocent... He's been detained at the Shiraz cinema camp...

KHURRAM

क्या चाहते हो?

How can I help you?

OLD MAN

छुड़वा दीजिए...

Please get him out ...

Khurram laughs.

KHURRAM

चाचा... मैं क्या जनरल कृश्णा राव हूँ कि नज़र उठायी
और आपका बेटा बाहर...
मैं उसे छुड़वा तो नहीं सकता पर बचा सकता हूँ... कैम्प से जेल में
तबादला करना होगा... जिसके लिए एफ.आई.आर. लगेगी... और
एफ.आई.आर. के लिए... इलज़ाम...

Uncle... I have no authority to free your boy.... I can't get him out but I can possibly save his life... We have to move him out of the camp and get him sentenced to a prison.... We'll need to file a formal report... We need to get him charged with a crime.

He takes a deep breath.

KHURRAM

इलज़ाम फॉल्स होगा, पर केस अदालत में तो आएगा,
मतलब कि डिसएपियरेंस का चांस - ज़ीरो...

It'll be a false charge.That would get him a hearing in a court. Once he is presented in court, he can't 'disappear'.

He calls the man closer.

KHURRAM

बताइए क्या लगवाना है... पब्लिक सेफ्टी एक्ट
या आर्म्स पोज़ेशन एक्ट?

So what shall it be... ? Public Safety Act... or Arms Possession Act?

The old man is confused.

CUT TO:

3 EXT. OUTSKIRTS OF SRINAGAR - LATER

A bulletproof Gypsy escorted by two other combat vehicles is moving on the outskirts of Srinagar.

INSIDE:

KHURRAM

दो केस हैं परवेज़ साहेब, एक आर्म्स पोज़ेशन एक पी.एस.ए...

Two cases, Parvez... one is arms possession and the other PSA...

Khurram hands over an envelope to Parvez.

KHURRAM

फिफ्टी...

Fifty...

Parvez smiles and keeps the packet aside. He brings out a plastic bag from the side.

PARVEZ

मेरे पास भी दो तोहफे हैं तुम्हारे लिए...

I have two gifts for you, too...

Khurram peeps inside the bag and takes out a bottle of Vodka. His smile broadens. He looks inside the bag to look for the second thing.

KHURRAM

और दूसरा तोहफा?

The second one?

PARVEZ

Chance... of a lifetime...

Khurram looks at him with questioning eyes.

CUT TO:

4 EXT. ABANDONED HOUSE - DAY

The Gypsy comes to a halt in front of an abandoned house in the woods. The house is surrounded by task force commandos.

Parvez walks towards the house accompanied by Khurram. He speaks to Khurram while acknowledging the salutes of the soldiers on the way.

PARVEZ

इख़वान को बढ़ाना है... इख़वान-उल-मुसलमीन...
weapon, paisa, power... सब कुछ...

We need to nourish the Ikhwaan... Ikhwaan-ul-Musalmeen... with weapons, funds, powers...

An officer comes out of the house.

OFFICER

Sir... Early morning operation...
तीनों सो रहे थे... एक भी गोली नहीं चलानी पड़ी...

Sir... early morning operation... all three were asleep... not a single shot fired...

Parvez smiles.

PARVEZ

तंज़ीम...?

Group...?

OFFICER

सोवियत अफगान वार की हड्डियाँ हैं सर... हरकत-उल-अंसार...

Leftovers from the Soviet Afghan war, sir... Harqat-ul-Ansar...

Parvez nods.

CUT TO:

5 INT. ABANDONED HOUSE

Parvez looks at the young captured militants sitting in a corner with their hands and feet tied together. Parvez picks up the Kalashnikov belonging to them.

PARVEZ

(to Khurram)

कितने लड़कों के केस हैं तुम्हारे पास?

How many cases do you have?

KHURRAM

कोई 75-80 होंगे.

About 75-80.

Parvez unlocks the gun.

KHURRAM

पर वो क्यों तैयार होंगे अपने लोगों के खिलाफ बंदूक उठाने के लिए...?

But why would they take up arms against their own?

PARVEZ

आज़ादी के लिए...

For freedom...

He opens fire on the opposite wall, making bulletholes on the door and windows. The glass comes crashing down. Khurram steps back from the sudden shock of the firing.

PARVEZ

क़ैद में आज़ादी बहुत याद आती है...

A man in prison will exchange anything
for his freedom...

Parvez gives the Kalashnikov back and takes a pistol from a commando standing by and unlocks it.

KHURRAM

हमें क्या मिलेगा?

What do we get?

PARVEZ

दिल्ली... और दिल्ली की बिल्ली...

Delhi...

Parvez chuckles, Khurram smiles. Suddenly, Parvez showers bullets at the captured militants, killing all three instantly.

PARVEZ

मरा हुआ मिलिटेन्ट एक लाख का है आजकल...

A dead militant is worth a lakh these days...

The other police officers start to dress up the crime scene, untying the ropes from the dead bodies and placing the guns in their hands.

PARVEZ

(to his subordinate)

Call the media.

He turns to Khurram.

PARVEZ

इखवाँ के मायने भूले तो नहीं?

Haven't forgotten the meaning
of Ikhwaan, have you?

Khurram smiles.

KHURRAM

भाई...

Brother...

Parvez smiles back.

CUT TO:

6 I/E. HIDEOUT - DOWNTOWN SRINAGAR - DAY

An old house somewhere in a heavily populated area of Srinagar, known as Downtown. The voice of a man screaming in pain.

INSIDE

DOCTOR HILAAL MEER, in his mid-fifties, administers an injection onto a bearded man's arm. He is IKHLAAKH LATIF, who's screaming in pain, holding his stomach. Two other men - REHMAT KHAN and ZAHOOR HUSSAIN - watch anxiously.

IKHLAAKH

आतते मौजे! आतते मौजे!

Mother! Oh mother!!

Three young men with Kalashnikovs slung over their shoulders are also present. Hilaal takes Zahoor and Rehmat aside.

HILAAL

(while preparing the injection)

बस बस कमांडर साहेब.

There, there, it will be ok, Commander.

It's severe अपेंडिसाइटिस... आपरशन करना पड़ेगा जल्द से जल्द.

It's a case of severe appendicitis. We need to operate immediately.

They look back at Ikhlaakh.

ZAHOOR

वो हमारी तहरीक का चेहरा है डॉ. साहब... अस्पताल ले जाने का चांस नहीं ले सकते हम.

He is the face of our struggle... We cannot risk going to the hospital.

HILAAL

चांस तो लेना पड़ेगा ज़हूर मियाँ... वर्ना कल दूरदर्शन पे समाचार सुनिएगा, कि कल रात कमाण्डर इख्लाख़ लतीफ पेट में अपेंडिक्स के धमाके से शहीद हो गया.

We will have to take the risk, Zahoor. Or tomorrow it will be reported... that Commander Ikhlaakh Latif died... after a terrifying explosion of his appendix.

A beat. They hold a look. Hilaal takes a deep breath.

HILAAL

मैं एम्बुलेन्स का इंतेज़ाम करके लेक के किनारे मिलूँगा एक घण्टे में...

I'll arrange an ambulance and will meet you at the lake in an hour.

Hilaal picks up his bag to leave.

REHMAT
पर ऑपरेशन करेंगे कहाँ आप?
But where will you operate?

Hilaal turns.

HILAAL
घर पे...
At home.

CUT TO:

7 EXT. DAL LAKE - BACK ALLEYS - LATER

Two young men furiously row a shikara through the inner backwater alleys. Ikhlaakh is lying in the boat covered by a blanket, the barrel of an AK47 sticking out beneath the blanket.

CUT TO:

8 EXT. ROADS IN OUTSKIRTS - DAY

The ambulance travels through the roads of the valley.

9 INT. SCHOOL CLASSROOM

GHAZALA, a pretty lady in her forties, stands at the front of the class reading out from a book. The students listen attentively.

- 'What is a home?' 'It is brothers and sisters...'

- And sisters. 'And fathers and mothers.'

- And mothers. 'It is unselfish acts and kindly sharing.'

- Sharing. 'And showing your loved ones you're always caring...'

- Caring.

'What is a house?'

Through the window she notices an ambulance stopping at the army checkpoint. She recognizes it. A beat.

CUT TO:

10 EXT. ARMY CHECKPOST OUTSIDE THE SCHOOL

The soldier-on-duty inspects the license and other papers of the young man driving. On the passenger seat is Dr Hilaal, whom the soldier recognizes.

SOLDIER
डॉक्टर साब कैसे हो?
Doctor, how are you?

HILAAL
अच्छा हूँ.
I am fine.

SOLDIER
देर बहुत हो गई आज?
You got delayed today...

HILAAL
एक ऑपरेशन है...
Another surgery...

SOLDIER
हाँ भाई डॉक्टर साब को जाने दो...
Let the doctor go...

CUT TO:

11 INT. SCHOOL CLASSROOM

Ghazala sees the soldier raising the barricade letting the ambulance pass.

She turns to her students and continues the lecture.

CUT TO:

12 EXT. TOWN - OUTSKIRTS OF ANANTNAG - DAY

The ambulance is parked in the courtyard of a nice double-storied house, a few hundred metres off the main road.

Children returning from school play in the lanes.

CUT TO:

13 INT. HILAAL'S HOME - KITCHEN - DAY

Surgical instruments are boiling in a pot. Ghazala stands facing the gas stove in the kitchen. The room is tense and silent, Ghazala has a sense of paranoia in her demeanour. She scratches at the back of her palm with her finger nail, peeling off the skin of a half-healed wound. Hilaal walks in with a bunch of other surgical tools in a tray. Ghazala stops scratching. He keeps the tray on the slab close to her. Ghazala starts putting the instruments from the boiling water into the tray.

HILAAL

आँच कम करे लें थोड़ी...

Lower the heat a bit...

She lowers the knob of the stove, Hilaal smiles.

HILAAL

अंदर की भी...

And the flames within you...

He touches her and immediately pulls back his hand.

HILAAL

उफ... आग लग जाएगी घर में...

They can burn this house down!

Ghazala looks at him.

GHAZALA

घर नहीं पूरा गाँव जलवा देंगे आप.

You will have the village burnt to ashes.

Hilaal is quiet. She looks in his eyes, straight.

GHAZALA

डॉक साहब... आप जानते हैं ना आप क्या कर रहे हैं?

Doctor... Can't you see what you have gotten into?

Hilaal starts to put instruments into the tray.

HILAAL

वही... जो एक डॉक्टर को करना चाहिए...

Yes. Exactly what a doctor should be doing.

Hilaal takes a few steps to leave.

GHAZALA

किस तरफ हैं आप?

Which side are you on?

He stops.

HILAAL

ज़िंदगी की...

I am for life...

He looks at her. They hold the look. A beat.

CUT TO:

14 INT. HILAAL'S HOME - ATTIC - LATER

Hilaal operates on Ikhlaakh using a table-tennis table for a surgeon's table. The militants work as paramedics, helping him, using cotton swabs and small towels to wipe the blood.

CUT TO:

15 INT. HILAAL'S HOME - STAIRCASE CORRIDOR - LATER

It's well into the night. Ghazala waits in the balcony under the attic. A noise in the drainage pipe. Blood-coloured water flushes out.

The young man comes down the steps with a large bowl full of bloody napkins and instruments. There is quite a lot of blood in the bowl. He hands it over to Ghazala and climbs back up to the attic.

Ghazala is left alone with the blood-filled bowl. Looking into it, a feeling of nausea overcomes her.

16 INT. BATHROOM - NIGHT

Ghazala throws up violently in the wash basin. She stops after a while and looks at herself in the mirror. The telephone rings outside.

17 INT. STUDY

Ghazala looks at the ringing telephone.

CUT TO:

18 EXT. AISHMUQAM VILLAGE - NIGHT

It's still dark outside. A convoy of army vehicles moves along a mountain road.

CUT TO:

19 EXT. AISHMUQAM VILLAGE - DAWN

The village is awash in a misty blue light before sunrise. The drone of motors grows closer. A long line of army trucks and Gypsies stops on the outskirts of the village. Columns of armed soldiers briskly jump out of the trucks and scatter through the fields circling the village. Several trucks and Gypsies move further into the village.

CUT TO:

20 INT. AISHMUQAM VILLAGE - MOSQUE - LATER

The sleepy muezzin is seated in front of a microphone. The lieutenant beside him.

MUEZZIN

सलाम आलेकुम मैं गुल खान बोल रहा हूँ. फौज ने cordon-and-search का आर्डर दिया है गाँव में, लिहाज़ा तमाम मर्द और नौजवान लड़के दस मिनट में स्कूल के मैदान में जमा हो जाएँ। औरतें और बच्चे घरों में ही रह सकते हैं... फौज ने cordon-and-search का हुकुम दिया है गाँव में, लिहाज़ा तमाम मर्द और नौजवान लड़के दस मिनट में स्कूल के मैदान में जमा हो जाएँ...

Salam alaikum! This is Gul Khan. The army has cordoned off the village. It is a search operation... Requesting every man and every boy to assemble in the school grounds immediately. Women and children may remain home.

The announcement blares from the mosque speakers. A few lights flicker on inside houses, and within moments lights in almost all the houses are on.

CUT TO:

21 INT. HILAAL'S HOME - BEDROOM

A startled Ghazala wakes up hearing the distant sound of the announcement. She violently shakes Hilaal who sleeps next to her.

GHAZALA

हिलाल... क्रैकडाउन.... गाँव में क्रैकडाउन हो रहा है!

Hilaal! There's a crackdown in our village.

Hilaal gets up immediately and walks to the window. He sees soldiers taking positions in the alleys. He is shocked.

22 EXT. AISHMUQAM VILLAGE - DAWN

The announcement continues as the sun rises.

MUEZZIN

(off-screen)

सब मर्द और नौजवान लड़के दस मिनट में अस्पताल के
मैदान में जमा हो जाएं...

Requesting every man and every boy to assemble in
the school grounds immediately.

Soldiers move into formation creating an inner circle around the village.

MUEZZIN

औरतें, लड़कियाँ और छोटे बच्चे घरों में रह सकते हैं.

Women and children may remain home.

CUT TO:

23 INT. HILAAL'S HOME - ATTIC

Hilaal hands over some fruits and water as he instructs the two men and Ikhlaakh.

HILAAL

यह नास्ते के पहले, यह नास्ते के बाद और यह दोपहर में... दर्द ज्यादा हो तो यह इंजेक्शन.

Take this before meals, this afterwards. If the pain gets worse, inject this.

He hands over medicines to one of the boys. He looks at Ikhlaakh. They look at each other for a long moment. Hilaal holds Ikhlaakh's hands in his hands.

IKHLAAKH

खोदयूस हवलेह...

Khodayus Hawaleh... Leaving you in the care of God.

CUT TO:

24 INT. HILAAL'S HOME - STAIRCASE CORRIDOR

Ghazala watches as Hilaal hides the collapsible staircase. Now it seems just like a ceiling wall, with nothing above.

25 INT. HILAAL'S HOME

Hilaal takes out his ID card from a drawer and heads towards the exit. Ghazala stands near the door, scratching the back of her palm with her nail. He stops, their eyes meet. A beat.

HILAAL

अगर उन्हें ज़रा सा भी शक हुआ तो कोई नहीं बचेगा...
ना तुम ना मैं...

Be careful... If they suspect something... no one will survive. Neither you... nor I.

Hilaal turns to go, she whispers from behind.

GHAZALA

और हैदर...?

What about Haider?

Hilaal stops, his eyes turn to a photograph of him and a young boy, making faces for the camera. A smile emerges in his eyes.

HILAAL

उसका हामी हो खुदा... और खुदा है...
उसका हाफिज़... खुदा रहेगा...

God is his guardian. He will take care of him...

Hilaal opens the door and walks out with his ID card held in his raised hands. Ghazala watches from a distance.

26 EXT. AISHMUQAM VILLAGE - DAWN

Armed soldiers on both sides of the road leading to the hospital compound.

Ghostlike figures in pherans slowly make their way through the lanes without uttering a word to each other.

Every villager, like a well-rehearsed actor, is carrying his identity card in his hand. Hilaal, a proud man walking erect, with dignity, standing out among the villagers.

Women peep from windows while their sons, husbands, brothers and fathers walk by, supervised by armed soldiers.

CUT TO:

27 EXT. AISHMUQAM VILLAGE - HOSPITAL GROUND-LATER

The ground is fully covered by a sea of people squatting on every inch of the ground. Some faces are tense; some are resigned.

28 INT. HILAAL'S HOME-ATTIC

Wincing in pain Ikhlaakh peeps through a slit in the attic. All he can see is army vehicles.

29 INT. HILAAL's HOME

Ghazala cautiously opens the door and walks nervously past the soldiers to a neighbour's house. She joins a circle of women sitting in the courtyard of the house. The women sit close to each other, their faces tense, looking out towards the soldiers in anticipation and anxiety.

CUT TO:

30 EXT. AISHMUQAM VILLAGE - HOSPITAL GROUND - LATER

An armoured Gypsy, heavily guarded by armed soldiers, is parked right outside the hospital building. Behind a grilled window a man in an army uniform is seated, his face is covered with a black hooded mask, only his eyes can be seen. He is the MUKHBIR (informer).

An identification parade is under way. A major sits at the side with a lieutenant conducting the procedure.

The villagers are taking turns passing in front of the Mukhbir. Two young men stand nervously in front of him. Hilaal flinches as he hears cries coming out of the adjacent building, where arrested men are being tortured.

'Khodayo Bachav!'

Save me.. Oh, Lord!

'Nahin Pata Sir!'

I don't know!!

The first young man passes by the Mukhbir. We see anticipation on the faces of villagers in the ground, the relief in their eyes as the second young man passes by the Mukhbir safely.

Hilaal stands in front of the Mukhbir. A long tense moment. The Mukhbir raises his hand.

CUT TO:

31 INT. HILAAL'S HOME - ATTIC

One of the men notices something outside.

YOUNG MAN

इख़्लाख़ साहेब... ये लोग क्या कर रहे हैं?

What are they doing?

Ikhlaakh moves over to have a look. He sees soldiers uncoiling some wires around the house perimeter.

IKHLAAKH

उन्हें पता है मैं यहाँ हूँ... कलाशनिकोव ला मेरा...

They know I am here. Bring me the Kalashnikov.

The two men are startled. Despite the pain in his abdomen, Ikhlaakh takes out and puts back the magazine, locks and unlocks, prepares his Kalashnikov.

IKHLAAKH

तुम दोनों चाहो तो सरेंडर कर दो...

You guys can surrender if you wish...

Both young men look at each other and nod their heads negatively. Ikhlaakh smiles.

IKHLAAKH

20-25 साथ लेके जाएंगे... इंशाअल्लाह...

We'll take down 20-25 along with us,
God willing...

CUT TO:

32 INT. HILAAL'S HOME

A lieutenant leads three soldiers stealthily into the house.

33 EXT. HILAAL'S HOME

The house is surrounded by army vehicles at a distance. The Major looks through binoculars into the windows for any sign of movement. He picks up a megaphone and speaks.

MAJOR

इख्लाख़ लतीफ... तुम्हें भारतीय कानून के तहत अपने आप
को बचाने का पूरा मौका दिया जायेगा... हथियार अन्दर छोड़ के बाहर
आ जाओ... You don't have a chance...
सरेंडर कर दो... वर्ना मारे जाओगे!

Ikhlaakh Latif... Surrender yourself...You will get a trial... Lay down your weapons and come out. You don't have a chance... Surrender or die!

CUT TO:

34 EXT. HILAAL'S NEIGHBOUR'S HOUSE. DAY.

Ghazala is standing anxiously on the edge of the circle of women in the courtyard. Her eyes are moving between looking at her house and looking towards the soldiers circling it. She scratches at the back of her palm with the finger nail. Suddenly, a cry almost escapes her lips. She is startled to see a group of soldiers pushing a handcuffed Hilaal towards the Major. Hilaal sees Ghazala and their eyes meet for a moment. A beat.

35 INT. HILAAL'S HOME - STAIRCASE CORRIDOR

The soldiers stand right below the hidden attic. A silent survey of the walls. A tiny crevice is noticed.

36 INT. HILAAL'S HOME-ATTIC

Ikhlaakh sees the soldiers through the slit. Ikhlaakh and his boys have their guns pointed downwards, ready to fire.

37 INT. HILAAL'S HOME - STAIRCASE CORRIDOR

The soldiers point their guns upwards. Both teams stand still, waiting. A tense stand-off.

The lieutenant signals his soldiers to move on the count of three. He raises his hand... One... Two...

Before he reaches 'three', an onslaught of bullets come piercing through the wooden planks above them, immediately killing one of the soldiers and injuring the lieutenant.

38 EXT. HILAAL'S HOME

The Major reacts to the sounds of the bullets. Tense soldiers take aim and await commands.

39 INT. HILAAL'S HOME - STAIRCASE CORRIDOR

The firing overwhelms the soldiers. One provides covering fire as the other assists the injured lieutenant with the dead soldier's body. They retreat.

40 INT. HILAAL'S HOME - STAIRCASE CORRIDOR

Ikhlaakh and his men have made their way down to the corridor window. They fire at the soldiers.

41 EXT. HILAAL'S HOME

Soldiers retaliate to the firing. The Major rushes towards the lieutenant who's receiving first aid.

They both look at the dead soldier inside the van. Angry, the Major looks towards the house.

42 EXT. HILAAL'S HOME - LATER

The stand-off continues with sporadic firing every few minutes. A handcuffed Hilaal is brought to the Major.

A soldier with a small remote positions himself near the

Major and nods. A beat. The Major looks back at Hilaal and whispers.

MAJOR

फाइर!

Fire!

At the click of a button, the explosives blow up the base of the house. Hilaal cries in horror. The Major signals to the men with rocket launchers.

Within seconds two rockets fly into the attic and the first floor completely annihilating the structure. What's left of the house goes up in flames.

FADE TO BLACK.

ON BLACK : TITLE APPEARS.

HAIDER

FADE IN :

43 EXT. A BUS ON THE MOUNTAIN ROADS - DAY

A young man looks through the window of a bus into nothingness - HAIDER MEER, in his early twenties. His eyes are heavy, red, as if after hours of crying.

CUT TO:

44 EXT. ARMY CHECK POST - JAWAHAR TUNNEL - DAY

The bus slowly stops, he looks outside, it has halted behind a couple of other vehicles. It's some kind of a road block. A distant sound of gun firing can be heard on the soundtrack.

A soldier gets into the bus holding an automatic weapon.

SOLDIER

आई.डी. और सामान लेकर बाहर लाईन बनाइए सब लोग...

Everybody line up outside with your IDs and bags.

There is a murmur of disappointment among the passengers.

CUT TO:

45 EXT. ARMY CHECK POST JAWAHAR TUNNEL - LATER

Haider stands in a queue with his rucksack on the shoulders as soldiers frisk people after checking their IDs and luggage.

A soldier checks Haider's ID as a south Indian-looking officer, LIEUTENANT NAGARAJAN, stands close to the post, observing.

SOLDIER

कहाँ जा रहे हो.

Where are you going?

HAIDER

श्रीनगर.

Srinagar.

SOLDIER

कहाँ से आ रहे हो?

You are coming from?

HAIDER

अलीगढ़.

Aligarh.

SOLDIER

क्या करते हो वहाँ?

What do you do there?

HAIDER

पढ़ता हूँ.

I'm a student.

SOLDIER

आई.डी.

Your identity card?

Haider takes out his university ID from his wallet. The lieutenant takes it from him and studies it. It is from the History department of Aligarh Muslim University. Haider is an MPhil student.

LIEUTENANT NAGARAJAN

क्या subject है research का?

What do you research?

HAIDER

ब्रितानिया काबिज़ हिन्द में इंकलाबी शोहरा.

Revolutionary poetry in British India.

LIEUTENANT NAGARJAN

वाट?

What?

HAIDER

Revolutionary poetry in British India.

The lieutenant smiles. Haider smiles back coldly.

LIEUTENANT NAGARJAN

कहाँ के रहने वाले हो?

Where are you from?

HAIDER

इस्लामाबाद.

Islamabad.

All the soldiers turn and look at him as if he has dropped a bomb.

CUT TO:

46 INT. ARMY CHECK-POST ROOM - LATER

Haider sits alone inside a small room of the check post. He looks out through a small window. From the opposite end a Maruti 800 drives in from afar. He recognizes it. The soldiers get alert. They run and stop it at a distance.

A petite, beautiful, yet forceful girl in a pink salwar kameez, a long beige coat and a woollen cap, hanging a press card from her neck, comes out. This is ARSHIA LONE. She shows her press ID and the press sticker of Kashmir Post *pasted on her car.*

CUT TO:

47 I/E. ARMY CHECK-POST ROOM

A soldier walks in. Haider looks at him.

SOLDIER

चलो.

Come.

Haider comes out. Arshia, who was chatting with the lieutenant, turns. Their eyes meet, a look of longing and desire. She walks up to him, close, holding herself from hugging him. A beat.

ARSHIA
(whispers)
मारूँगी तुम्हें!
I'll thrash you!

Haider smiles. The lieutenant walks up to them.

LIEUTENANT NAGARJAN
दिल में कशमीर और ज़बान पे इस्लामाबाद...
Your love for Kashmir... is expressed as Islamabad?

HAIDER
जी?
What?

Arshia butts in.

ARSHIA

सर... अनन्तनाग को इस्लामाबाद भी कहते हैं यहाँ...

Sir, Islamabad is another name for Anantnag.

LIEUTENANT NAGARJAN

(smiles)

I know... पर हमारे लिए सिर्फ एक ही इस्लामाबाद है...

उस तरफ...

But for us... there's just one Islamabad... across the mountains in Pakistan...

He hands over a diary to Haider.

LIEUTENANT NAGARJAN

By the way... nice poetry.

Haider is embarrassed.

LIEUTENANT NAGARJAN

Be careful with such beautiful inspiration. Okay?

Arshia smiles at Haider. Haider smiles back broadly, faking the delight.

CUT TO:

48 EXT. ROADS IN OUTSKIRTS - DAY

Haider looks outside the window as Arshia tries to explain herself.

ARSHIA

क़सम से यार हैदर... वो मसाला डोसा मान ही नहीं रहा था... मैंने

कहा सर वो मिलिटेन्ट नहीं है पोएट है, हमारी शादी होने वाली है, उसने कहा सबूत? तो मैने कहा डायरी पढ़ लिजिए... सारी पोएट्री मेरे लिए लिखी है बचपन से...

I swear, Haider, that Masala Dosa wouldn't budge. I told him that you are a poet, not a militant. And we are engaged to be married. He wanted proof. I told him to read your diary. All the poems have been written for me... since we were kids.

No reaction from Haider. She turns a bend and stops the car by the road outside a village, surrounded by empty fields. She hugs him tight.

ARSHIA

(whispers)

और वैसे मैंने झूठ बोला क्या?

Wasn't a lie, was it?

A beat. Haider's voice starts choking as he speaks.

HAIDER

आर्मी ओबुजी को उठा कर ले गई और किसी ने दो हफ्ते तक कुछ नहीं बताया मुझे...

The army arrested my father and nobody mentioned a thing to me for two weeks.

He comes out of the embrace and looks at her.

HAIDER

रोज एस.टी.डी. पे बात करते थे मुझसे...

We spoke every day over the phone...

She looks down.

HAIDER

तुम, मौजे, चाचा सबने मिलकर धोखा दिया मुझे.

you... mother... uncle... everyone lied to me...

ARSHIA

तुम dissertation बीच में छोड़कर वापस आ जाते... गज़ाला चाची ने क़सम दी थी कुरान की...

You'd abandon your dissertation in the middle of the semester and return... Your mother made me promise not to tell you...

Haider looks away.

ARSHIA

I am sorry.

Arshia presses his hand gently, he keeps looking out.

CUT TO:

49 EXT. SRINAGAR ROADS - DAY

They drive into town, passing through army bunkers, armoured vehicles on every corner, soldiers posted on roads at the distance of every 50 metres, holding automatic weapons. They cross a half-burnt structure. Haider is shocked.

ARSHIA

तुम्हारे जाने के बाद बहुत कुछ बदल गया है यहाँ... नया लतीफ़ा सुना तुमने? दो महीने बाद इलेक्शन हो रहे हैं...

Thing have changed since you were here last... Did you hear the new joke... elections are due in two months...

HAIDER

लतीफ़ों में अक्सर सच्चाई छुपी रहती है...

There is often truth in jest...

ARSHIA

हैदर... तुम कह रहे हो यह? You've changed, यार... अलीगढ़ में किसी हिन्दुस्तानी लड़की के चक्कर में तो नहीं पड़ गए हो?

Haider... are you serious? You've changed... Haven't fallen in love with an Indian girl back in Aligarh, have you?

Haider faintly smiles.

HAIDER

कहाँ जा रहे हैं हम?

Where are we going?

ARSHIA

मौजे के पास...

To your mother.

HAIDER

है वो कहाँ?

Where is she?

ARSHIA

चाचा के यहाँ.

At uncle Khurram's place.

Haider puts his hand on the steering wheel.

HAIDER

मुझे अपने घर जाना है.

I want to go home.

Arshia stops the car and looks straight into his eyes.

ARSHIA

तुम्हारे घर में... घर जैसा कुछ बचा नहीं है हैदर...

There isn't a much of a home left in what remains...

Tears form in her eyes and she looks away.

CUT TO:

50 EXT. HILAAL'S HOME - LATER

Haider stands shocked opposite the burnt, torn-down structure. It's beyond his belief seeing what's left of the house he grew up in. Arshia stands behind giving him space.

51 INT. HILAAL'S HOME

The foundation walls of the structure are still in place. As he walks through the house, he sees charred remains of the furniture, the staircase, etc.

Flashes of his childhood appear before him as he walks through the house.

-Young Haider and Hilaal engrossed in a serious table-tennis match in the attic as Ghazala calls out to them for lunch.

- Dawn, young Haider crawls into bed in between Ghazala and Hilaal snuggling up to them inside the blanket.

- Hilaal displays a ten-rupee note to a sheepish young Haider.

HILAAL

गुलों में रंग भरे बाद-ए-नौ बहार चले...

Let the petals fill with colour... Let the breeze ruffle the spring...

He urges Haider on to finish the poem, the boy thinks hard.

HILAAL

बाद-ए-नौ बहार चले...

Let the breeze ruffle the spring...

Suddenly he blurts out the rest of the poem and quickly grabs the note.

HAIDER

चले भी आओ कि गुलशन का करोबार चले...

Come along, my love...

Awake the garden to life...

-Young Haider rushes to brush Hilaal's shoes as Hilaal leaves for office in the morning.

Flashback ends:

Haider bends down to pick a video cassette, something catches his attention on the ground. A photo-frame housing a photo of Hilaal, Ghazala and Haider.

He falls to his knees, crying in disbelief as he picks up the photo. Arshia places her hand on his shoulder, comforting him.

CUT TO:

52 EXT. HILAAL'S HOME

LIYAQAT PARVEZ LONE, in his early thirties, drives by in a police jeep. He notices Arshia's car and instructs the driver to stop.

LIYAQAT

एक मिनट रूको.

Stop the jeep.

The jeep stops.

LIYAQAT

अर्शिया की गाड़ी यहाँ क्या कर रही हैं?

What is Arshee's car doing here?

The driver shakes his head.

53 INT. HILAAL'S HOME

Haider is crying in Arshia's arms. She comforts him. He hugs her tight.

ARSHIA

हैदर... अपने आप से लड़ना बंद करो... रो लो... रो लो...

Don't fight it......You can cry... You can cry...

...Please.

She wipes the tears from his face and kisses him on his lips. He looks at her, they kiss again. This time a long passionate one.

54 EXT. HILAAL'S HOME

Liyaqat gets out of the jeep and walks towards the house. He touches the hood of Arshia's car, it's still warm.

CUT TO:

55 INT. HILAAL'S HOME

Haider and Arshia still in each other's arms.

LIYAQAT

(off-screen)

तो ये है तुम्हारा इम्पोर्टेन्ट इन्टरव्यू... इसलिए तुम एयरपोर्ट नहीं आ पा रही थी मुझे सी ऑफ करने...

Now that is quite an interview! Of course, you couldn't drop me at the airport.

The couple breaks out of the embrace.

ARSHIA

भाई...

Brother...

Liyaqat angrily walks up to them and pushes Haider hard; he bangs into a broken cupboard. Liyaqat holds him by the collar.

LIYAQAT

अब कभी मैंने तुझे इसके आस-पास भी देखा तो तू डिसएपियर हो जाएगा, अपने बाप की तरह... समझा? किसकी तरह?

Mark my words. If I ever see you around her... you will disappear... Just like your father. You get me? Like your...

Before he can finish his sentence, Haider pushes him back. Liyaqat bangs into the opposite wall. He gets up and runs towards Haider like an animal. Arshia comes in the middle.

ARSHIA

भाई... नहीं...

Brother... listen...

Liyaqat stops.

LIYAQAT

अर्शी... हट जा.

Arshee, move aside.

ARSHIA

आप जाइए यहाँ से.

Leave us! Please.

Liyaqat looks at Haider and then Arshia. A beat. He suddenly grabs her by the wrist and drags her out as she protests.

ARSHIA

भाई... हाथ छोड़ो मेरा.

Let go of my hand.

He drags her out and starts looking for the key inside her bag. The elderly driver of the police jeep comes to him.

MAQSOOD

लियाकत बेटा फ्लाइट छूट जाएगी.

Liyaqat you'll miss your flight.

Liyaqat finds the key and looks at him.

LIYAQAT

छूट गयी.

I've already missed it.

He pushes Arshia inside the car, comes to the driver seat, starts the car and zooms away.

CUT TO:

56 INT. PARVEZ'S HOME - LIVING ROOM - LATER

Arshia sits on a sofa and sobs, while knitting a sweater angrily. Parvez in his police uniform sits opposite and listens to Liyaqat quietly, who paces up and down.

LIYAQAT

मेरी सुनते कहाँ थे आप, जो इसके दिल में आया आपने करने दिया, अब देख लीजिए नतीजा.

You never heard my caution. You never listen to me. You let her do as she pleases. And this is what it has come to.

He stops and looks at Arshia.

LIYAQAT

घर से बाहर कदम नहीं रखेगी ये.

She won't leave the house.

ARSHIA
(whispers, sobbing and knitting)
नौकरी नहीं छोड़ूँगी मैं.
I will not stop working.

Liyaqat looks at Parvez.

PARVEZ
ठीक है... पर अब हैदर से मत मिलना बेटा.
Alright... but you have to stop seeing Haider.

She looks at her father, her eyes full of tears.

PARVEZ
लकी ठीक कह रहा है... डॉक्टर साहब के बाद बड़ी मुश्किल होगी अब उसे... मिलिटेन्ट फैमिली वालों को ना पासपोर्ट मिल सकता है, ना आसानी से सरकारी नौकरी... तुम जानती हो...
Lucky is right about it. After the doctor's arrest, his world is out of joint. He is a marked man. The families of militants become outcasts. They can't get passports. They can't get government jobs. You know how it is.

Liyaqat picks up the Quran kept on a wooden table over the prayer rug.

LIYAQAT
क़सम खा.
Swear by the Quran.

She looks at Liyaqat.

LIYAQAT

हाथ रख.

Place your hand on it.

She suddenly gets up and walks towards her room.

LIYAQAT

अर्शी...

Arshee...

She shuts the door and bolts it from inside. Liyaqat knocks angrily from outside.

LIYAQAT

अर्शी... दरवाज़ा खोल...

Arshee... Open the door...

Parvez comes from behind and puts his hand on Liyaqat's shoulder.

PARVEZ

2 बजे एक और फ्लाइट है बंगलौर की वाया दिल्ली.

There's another flight to Bangalore via Delhi at two.

LIYAQAT

मुझे नहीं जाना.

I don't want to go.

PARVEZ

पागल है... नहीं जाना नहीं जाना...

Don't be a fool... 'Don't want to go...'

PARVEZ

इतने बड़े मल्टीनेशनल की सर्विस. मज़ाक है क्या... बच्ची है वो... मैं समझा लूँगा... ला मैं क़सम खाता हूँ...

You don't turn down a big break with a major corporation. A man is not frivolous about his work. She has the mind of a child... - I'll speak to her.

He keeps his hand on the Quran.

PARVEZ

चल अब चल...

Here... I swear by the Quran...

Parvez hugs Liyaqat.

PARVEZ

गुस्सा बहुत करता है तू... बंगलौर में जा के वह करना... अमा वह है ना... श्री श्री रवि शंकर जी... उनका कोर्स, क्या नाम है...

You're too short tempered... When you get to Bangalore join that course... that one... by Sri Sri Ravi Shankar...

Liyaqat laughs softly.

LIYAQAT

The Art of Living.

He starts leading him out.

PARVEZ

हाँ वह करना... और दोस्तियाँ ज़रा सोच समझ के बनाना वहाँ. हाथ सब से मिलाना मगर दिल सिर्फ अपनों से. और जब तक हो सके तो

छुपाना कि तुम कहाँ से हो... आजकल हिन्दुस्तानियों को हर कशमीरी में टेरोरिस्ट नज़र आता है...

Yes that one... be careful who you make friends with. Be friendly to everyone... but befriend only a few... and as much as possible don't tell anyone where you're from... Nowadays Indians see a terrorist in every Kashmiri.

Liyaqat nods.

CUT TO:

57 EXT. PARVEZ'S HOME - PORCH - LATER

Liyaqat leaves in the car. Parvez waves goodbye. He turns to see Arshia standing at the door step still knitting the sweater. Their eyes meet. He walks up to her, she is avoiding eye contact.

PARVEZ

ये मेरा मफ्लर, कब पूरा होगा?

When will this muffler be ready?

ARSHIA

(still looking down)

सर्दियों से पहले...

before the winters, for sure...

Parvez pulls her face by the chin.

PARVEZ

कितनी गर्मियों से यही बोल रही है तू... चे शक कमीन...

I hear this every summer... you brat...

Arshia smiles, he hugs her.

ARSHIA

इस बार... ज़रूर...

This time for sure..

Parvez caresses her hair lovingly.

PARVEZ

बेटा... वक़्त फिर गया है... हैदर से अब हमदर्दी तो मुमकिन है... मुहब्बत नहीं.

Times are bad sweetheart... You can sympathize with Haider... but you can't be in love with him..

Arshia's face has a grim expression.

CUT TO:

58 INT. KHURRAM'S HOME

Haider gets down from an auto outside a small bungalow located in a modest middle-class locality in Srinagar. The name plate on the bungalow reads 'Khurram Meer - B.A. LLB - Advocate High Court'.

Haider opens the gate and enters, an old man comes out of the corridor. A face Haider recognizes and knows well. The old man hugs him tight, his eyes are moist.

59 INT. KHURRAM'S HOME - LIVING ROOM

Haider walks through the corridor, photographs of his father and uncle on the walls. He hears a faint singing voice of a male, coming from the other end. He follows the voice.

Through the thin wooden curtain he sees Khurram singing a Kashmiri song holding a cup of tea in between his palms. The smoke flowing out of the cup in the backdrop of the evening sunlight makes the atmosphere magical. Ghazala seems rather cheerful and happy. She is trying to hold her amusement as Khurram sings.

KHURRAM
(in Kashmiri)
Roash-e-walo miyanih dilbaro…
Poshan bahara yoorih valo…

She suddenly bursts into laughter.

KHURRAM
क्या हुआ?
Why are you laughing?

GHAZALA

कितना बेसुरा गाते हो तुम...

You are so out of tune...

Haider freezes in his tracks. He notices a certain look in his mother's eyes, a look he has never seen before.

KHURRAM

370 सालों से गुज़ारिश कर रहे हैं आपसे... कॉलेज के दिनों से...
... शागिर्द बना लें हमें अपना... उस्तानी बन जाएं हमारी... पर आप
मानती कहाँ हैं... बाबीजान...

Be my master! I have been begging you to
teach me since college... Be my master...
And you look away...

Ghazala giggles.

KHURRAM

अच्छा, आप गाइए...

Why don't you sing?

Ghazala shakes her head to say no. Khurram presses her knee.

KHURRAM

गाइए ना... प्लीज़...

Please sing...

Ghazala picks up her cup and starts to sing while blowing the vapours away from the cup. Khurram slowly gets up and starts to gently dance along. His steps have a kind of sweetness of the local folk dance. Ghazala is amused and gets into giggles in between her singing.

Haider enters the room pushing the see-through wooden curtain aside.

Ghazala casually turns with a smile, still humming. She stops, seeing Haider. She suddenly becomes pale and whispers to herself.

GHAZALA

जाना...

My dear...

Khurram looks at her and follows her gaze. He is startled to see Haider standing behind. He gets up trying to gather himself.

KHURRAM

हैदर... मेरी जान... कब आया तू? खबर भी नहीं की...

Haider! When did you arrive? You didn't even let us know...

He opens his arms to embrace his nephew. Haider walks past him towards his mother. A beat. Ghazala tries to behave normally but stutters and stammers.

GHAZALA

जाना... कितना थका लग रहा है... चाय पिएगा? मैंने बनाई है...

You're looking so tired... will you have tea... I've made it...

She hurriedly pours some tea and brings the cup to him. He keeps looking at her silently. Ghazala pats her forehead.

GHAZALA

पागल हूँ मैं... भूल ही गयी कि तू चाय नहीं पीता कॉफी पीता है...

My dear... You've lost so much weight... You've grown a beard too...

She puts the cup back and looks back at him lovingly. She gently brushes his hair.

GHAZALA

Thesis लिख दी तूने? हम?

Completed your dissertation?

Haider is silent. Her voice starts to shake.

GHAZALA

तू कुछ बोलता क्यूँ नहीं? हम... बोल ना... कुछ तो...

Why are you so quiet? Why the silence? My dear...

Tears start forming in her eyes. She suddenly hugs him and starts crying. He doesn't move an inch, his hands dangling down, not moving to embrace her.

KHURRAM

क़यामत का दौर गुज़रा है हैदर... मगर यह सबर का वक़्त है...
कुरान-ए-पाक में लिखा है, इन-अल्लाह-हा-माज़-सबिरीन...

These are hard times. It's a time for patience.The Quran tells us God is with the patient.

Khurram comes forward to put his hand on Haider's shoulder.

KHURRAM

मैने पिटीशन डाली है कोर्ट में... परवेज साहब भी मालूम कर रहे हैं किस कैम्प में रखा है... थोड़ा वक़्त लगेगा मगर इंशाह-अल्लाह सब ठीक हो जाएगा...

I've filed a petition in court... It will take some time... But God-willing, all will be fine soon...

Haider whispers to Ghazala who still holds her.

HAIDER

लगता तो नहीं...

It doesn't look like it though...

She pulls herself back to look at him. Her face full of tears.

KHURRAM

मतलब?

What do you mean?

HAIDER

(to Khurram)

बहुत खुश नज़र आ रहे हैं आप लोग ओबुजी के जाने से...

The two of you seem quite happy... with my father's disappearance...

GHAZALA

क्या?

What?

Haider raises his voice a bit.

HAIDER

(to Ghazala)

बहुत खुश नज़र आ रहे हैं आप लोग ओबुजी के जाने से...

The two of you seem quite happy... with my father's disappearance.

A shocking silence echoes in the room. Khurram tries to save the situation.

KHURRAM

हैदर... पागल हो गया है तू... क्या बोल रहा है?

Haider... Have you lost it? What are you saying?

Haider cuts him in between.

HAIDER

वही जो देख रहा हूँ...

I will repeat what my eyes can see!

He turns towards Ghazala.

HAIDER

ये छुप-छुप के नाचना गाना पहले भी होता था कि अभी शुरू हुआ है...
ओबुजी के बाद...

Has your musical been on for a while? Or did this romantic production begin... after father's disappearance?

Ghazala suddenly slaps him hard. A beat. Haider turns and walks out towards the exit. Ghazala follows.

GHAZALA

I am sorry... Haider... मेरी बात सुन
Haider... I am sorry.

Haider walks in silence.

GHAZALA

हैदर... मैं सब समझाऊँगी तुझे.

Haider... I will explain everything to you...

Haider opens the main door and walks out.

GHAZALA

हैदर वापस आ जा... कर्फ्यू लगने वाला है पागल...

Haider... Come back... It is time for curfew now.

Haider keeps walking on the road with his rucksack on his shoulders trying his best to hold his tears inside.

GHAZALA
(screams)
जाना...
My dear...

Khurram comes to her from behind.

GHAZALA
आर्मी वाले उसे भी ले जाएंगे...
प्लीज़... रोक लो उसे...
The army will grab him too... Please stop him!

KHURRAM
कुछ नहीं होगा बाबी जान... आप अंदर चलें...
Nothing will happen to him. Come inside.

She cries more.

GHAZALA
नहीं... प्लीज़ बचा लो उसे...
Please get him back.

Khurram touches her elbow with concern.

KHURRAM
मैं हूँ ना... बाबी जान... मैं हूँ...
I'll take care of it. Don't worry.

He takes her inside.

CUT TO:

60 EXT. SRINAGAR - DAY

In a market area of the city, an awkward-looking stand-alone structure has a sign in front that says.

Salman & Salman video: all types VHS cassettes available.

On the shop front we see a few small posters. (Maine Pyar Kiya. Deewana Mastana.) *And a faded poster:* Lion of the Desert.

On the soundtrack, we hear a hit cheesy Bollywood song.

61 INT. SALMAN & SALMAN VIDEO SHOP - INNER ROOM

Close-up of a television on which grainy visuals of the same song play, in which Salman Khan, sporting a mullet hairstyle, is dancing his heart out.

We pull back, to see two young men in front of the TV, emulating the actor's moves with the utmost conviction. Both wearing jeans and a white vest, they also sport mullets identical to the movie star. They lip-sync the lyrics as they continue dancing with passion and admiration. They are SALMAN & SALMAN.

The room is full of smoke and the walls adorned with a few Salman Khan posters.

The phone rings, they hear it but keep dancing. A beat. It rings again.

Salman 1 picks up the cordless receiver, still dancing.

SALMAN 1

(into phone)

हेलो... हाँ जी... एक सेकण्ड...

Hello! Who do you want to speak to? Salman?
Just a moment.

He passes the receiver to Salman 2, who's still dancing.

SALMAN 1

सलमान... तेरे लिए...

Salman, this is for you.

SALMAN 2

(into phone)

हेलो, ... कौन चाहिए?... सलमान? एक सेकण्ड...

Hello! Who do you want to speak to?
This call is for you.

An irritated Salman 2 passes the receiver back to Salman 1.

SALMAN 2

तेरे लिए...

Hello...

As the song on TV reaches its crescendo. Salman 1 takes the receiver back but doesn't place it on his ear. Instead both Salmans vigorously tear off their vests as does the Salman on screen. The song ends, an irritated voice is heard in the receiver.

VOICE

हेलो... हेलो...

Hello... Hello...

Salman 1 realizes someone is still holding and speaks.

SALMAN 1

किससे बात करनी है यार तुझे?... सलमान से... सलमान से
(gestures towards TV) के सलमान से?
Who do you want to speak to?
With Salman, Salman... or Salman!?

Salman 1 listens to the caller while taking a drag from his cigarette.

SALMAN 1

मैं? मैं सलमान हूँ... और जिससे तूने पहले बात की वो सलमान था.
अब बताएगा कि तू कौन है...
Who am I? I am Salman. The person you spoke
to earlier was also Salman. And will you take the
trouble... to tell me who you are?

He suddenly coughs out smoke.

SALMAN 1

जेनाब... सॉरी जेनाब...
Sir... Sorry sir...

He puts his hand on the mouthpiece.

SALMAN 1

परवेज़ साहब...
Parvez sir...

Salman 2 snatches the receiver from him.

SALMAN 2

सलाम आलेकुम जेनाब. माफी जेनाब. सलमान जेनाब... हाँ जेनाब.

हैदर? जेनाब बहुत अच्छे से... बारहवीं तक साथ पढ़े हैं... कहाँ जेनाब?
बिल्कुल, आपका हुकुम जेनाब... सलाम अलिकुम जेनाब.

Hello sir... Sorry sir. Haider Meer. Yes, I know him very well. We did high school together.... Yes sir... Have a good day...

He puts the phone down and looks at Salman 1 angrily.

SALMAN 2

कोलेह चोटलेह! मैंने कहा था... फिल्म शुरू करने से पहले फोन का प्लग निकाल दे...

Fool! Didn't I tell you... to disconnect the phone before Brother Salman's movies...

Salman 1 bangs the remote of VCR on the bed. The video begins to play again, their attention goes back towards the screen. They start to dance again.

CUT TO:

62. EXT. MARKET ROAD - SRINAGAR - EVENING

An enraged and dejected Haider walks on the isolated road with his bag. A bakhtarbadh (armoured) vehicle drives up to him slowly from behind.

A masked and armed CRPF jawan with his upper body sticking out of the vehicle calls out to Haider.

CRPF JAWAN

रूको... कहाँ जा रहे हो?

Stop! Where are you going?

Haider snaps out of his trance-like walk and looks at the vehicle which stops beside him. The jawan comes out and walks to him.

CRPF JAWAN

बैग में क्या है?

What's in the bag?

Some other soldiers also come out of the vehicle.

CRPF JAWAN

आई कार्ड दिखाओ... और हाथ ऊपर करो...

Do you have an ID? And raise your hands...

Haider pulls out his ID from his wallet as he spreads his hands to be frisked. The jawan frisks him thoroughly.

Just then from the adjacent lane, Salman & Salman ride in on a motorcycle. They see Haider being frisked and ride up to him.

SALMAN 1

(to jawan)

जय हिन्द कैप्टन साहब.

Hello Captain.

The jawan recognizes the Salmans.

CRPF JAWAN

Salman and Salman.

Salman 2 gets off the bike and puts his hand over Haider's shoulder.

SALMAN 2

हैदर क्या हाल है भाई? कब आया?

Haider... How are you? When did you get back?

The jawan returns the ID card to Haider.

CRPF JAWAN

जानते हो इसे?

You know him?

SALMAN 2

मेजर साहब ये जान है हमारी... हमारी भाग्यश्री...

He's our sweetheart...

Salman 1 screams from the bike.

SALMAN 1

चल भाई! कर्फ्यू लगने वाला है... चलो, वर्ना कैम्प में मेजर पूछेगा, 'हम आपके हैं कौन?'

Come on, man... let's go... It's almost time for curfew... Or some Major will be welcoming us in a military camp.

Salman grabs Haider and takes him towards the bike. Haider sits on the bike sandwiched between the two Salmans. They ride away on the bike.

CUT TO:

63 EXT. DOWNTOWN - NIGHT

Downtown Kashmir at night. A few dogs wail on the street. A soldier flips a torch on and off from a bunker nearby. An old man walks hurriedly with a lantern in his hand. Thick coils of concertina wire surround the bunker. Haider's voice from the next scene fades in on the soundtrack.

HAIDER (v/o)

चुटज़पा.

C-H-U-T-Z-P-A-H.

64 I/E. SALMAN & SALMAN VIDEO SHOP - INNER ROOM - LATER

The TV is paused at the same dramatic scene from the Salman Khan film. The room is full of smoke of a Kashmiri hookah. All three look stoned.

HAIDER

चुटज़्पा हो रहा है यहाँ...

Chutzpah... It is what it is...

Salman 1 puts some charas into the pot.

SALMAAN 1

चुटज़्पा?

Chutzpah?

SALMAN 2

वो क्या है?

What is it?

Haider smokes, exhales hard, seems to choke, then smokes again.

HAIDER

एक बार एक लड़का अपने माँ-बाप का कत्ल करते पकड़ा गया. रंगे हाथ. कोर्ट में जज के सामने उसने कहा कि सज़ा देने में मुझ पर रहम

की नज़र रक्खी जाए. जज ने पूछा तूने अपने माँ-बाप का मर्डर किया है, रहम और तुझ पर… भला क्यों? लड़का बोला, जी यूँ कि अब मैं यतीम हूँ… अनाथ हूँ…

Once upon a time a boy was arrested for the murder of his parents. In the courtroom he sought a lenient sentence from the judge. Bewildered, the judge asked.. 'How do you expect mercy… after killing your own parents?' The boy replied... 'My Lord! Because I am an orphan now.'
Utter gall and brazenness!

Both the Salmans burst out laughing.

HAIDER

ये होता है चुटज़पा… हिब्रू ज़बान का लफ़्ज है…
That, my friend, is chutzpah. A Hebrew word.

SALMAAN 1

मगर अफ़स्पा और चूतियापा के कितने करीब है यार… आवाज और मानी दोनों में… अफ़स्पा चुटज़पा… चुटज़पा अफ़स्पा…
It does rhyme a bit with AFSPA... and all the bunkum it means. AFSPA... Chutzpah... Chutzpah... AFSPA...

Salman 2 shakes his head in agreement as Haider hits 'play' on a cassette player on the side. Mehdi Hassan's 'Gulon mei rang bhare' plays softly. Haider hums along.

HAIDER

गुलों में रंग भरे…
Let blossoms be colour-stained…

SALMAAN 2

अब तू क्या करेगा यहाँ?
What will you do now?

HAIDER

वही... चुटज़पा...

Chutzpah!

Both of them laugh again. Haider continues singing.

HAIDER

ढूँढूँगा... ओबुजी को.

I'll look for my father...

SALMAAN 1

कहाँ? कैम्पों में?

Where? In camps?

SALMAAN 2

क़ैदखानों में?

In prisons?

HAIDER

पूरा कशमीर क़ैदखाना है दोस्त... हर जगह जाऊँगा...

(sings aloud)

क़फस उदास है यारों सबा से कुछ तो कहो...

All of Kashmir is a prison my friends. I will look for him in every dark corner, on every unlit street. Everywhere.

CUT TO:

65 EXT. KHURRAM'S HOUSE - MORNING

A cold autumn morning. Ghazala stands in the balcony holding a cup of tea in her palms. Her eyes are stuck on the locked gate of the house.

An old newspaper man in a pheran and woollen cap carrying a bundle of newspapers stops on the street outside.

He tosses a copy of The Kashmir Post *over the gate.*

Ghazala opens the newspaper. The headline on the front page hits her like a bullet.

KHURRAM (v/o)
मैं बताने वाला था आपको...
I was going to tell you..

CUT TO:

66 INT. KHURRAM'S HOUSE - BEDROOM - LATER

Khurram still half-reads the newspaper headlines.

'Disappeared Doctor's Brother NDP candidate from Koshmar.'

A smiling photograph of Khurram with an NDP leader below the headline.

Ghazala scratches the back of her palm with her fingernail.

GHAZALA

कब? मरने के बाद?

When? After somebody kills you?

Khurram rubs his eyes.

KHURRAM

खामखा बात का बतंगड़ ना बनाइए बाबी-जान... ऐसा कुछ नहीं होगा.

Don't make a mountain of a molehill.. nothing will happen to me..

Ghazala turns around and cuts him in the middle.

GHAZALA

डॉक्टर साहब भी यही कहते थे. अब हिम्मत नहीं बची मुझमें... इस खौफ़ से नजात चाहिए...

The doctor used to say the same thing... I can't take it any more... I want to escape from this fear...

Khurram holds her hands as tears roll off her cheeks.

KHURRAM

यही तो एक रास्ता है नजात का बाबी-जान. यह इलेक्शन हमारा पुल-ए-सीरात है. जन्नत का आख़िरी इंतेहाँ.

This is the only way to escape... this election is our ticket out of here... it's our trial by fire...

KHURRAM

तलवार की धार का पुल, बाल से भी महीन, आग से भी गर्म... मगर पुल के पार जन्नत है बाबी-जान... दिल्ली है.

Once we're through... we move straight to Delhi... away from all this fear and violence.

She looks at him, eyes full of tears. He shakes his head.

CUT TO:

67 INT. DSP'S OFFICE- DAY

On a front wall of the police station is the fading graffiti:

'Catch Them By Their Balls, Their Hearts and Minds Will Follow.'

Inside:

Haider sits in front of Parvez.

PARVEZ

डॉक्टर साहब मेरे बहुत अज़ीज़ थे.

The doctor was one of my closest friends..

Haider looks at him sharply.

PARVEZ

अज़ीज़ हैं... देखो मैं तुम्हें कोई झूठा दिलासा नहीं देना चाहता... सच यह है आर्मी वाले हमारी बिल्कुल नहीं सुनते.

Is... not was... look I don't want to give you any false hope... but the truth is what powers do we the police have over the army?

Haider takes out some photocopied papers from his bag.

HAIDER

Armed Forces Special Powers Act, Rule 4 of section 5. Any person arrested and taken into custody under this Act shall be handed over to the officer in charge of the nearest police station with the least possible delay.

Haider looks at Parvez.

HAIDER

Least possible delay... आज 20 दिन हो गए है और उनका कुछ पता नहीं...

It's been twenty days and there's no word of him.

Parvez smiles sadly.

PARVEZ

सब कुछ कानून न हुआ होता तो यह हालत होती क्या कशमीर की? पंडित नेहरू ने लाल चौक में प्लेबिसाइट का वादा किया था, हुआ प्लेबिसाइट?

If things worked by the book... do you think Kashmir would have been the hell it is? Pandit Nehru promised Kashmiris a plebiscite with the world as his witness... What happened?

PARVEZ

प्लेबिसाइट तो छोड़ो, प्लेबिसाइट की पहली शर्त, डेमिलिटराइज़ेशन... वो तक पूरी नहीं की... ना पाकिस्तान ने, ना हिन्दुस्तान ने...

Let aside plebiscite... Even the first condition to plebiscite... demilitarization... did not happen.

He laughs at his own joke.

PARVEZ

(still laughing)

जब दो हाथी लड़ते हैं... तो घास ही कुचली जाती हैं...

Neither India, nor Pakistan...When two elephants fight... it is the grass that is trampled upon. A curse on both their houses!

Haider remains poker-faced.

HAIDER

मुझे एफ.आई.आर. दर्ज करना है...

I agree, Uncle...But I do want to file a formal report.

Parvez stops laughing and comes closer.

PARVEZ

फौज से दुशमनी मत लो बेटा. एफ.आई.आर. दर्ज करोगे तो उनके मिलने के चांसेज़ और कम हो जाएंगे...

Don't mess with the army, son. If you file a formal report... the chances of finding him will become even more bleak.

A beat on Haider.

PARVEZ

डॉक्टर साहब की सलामती इसी में है कि हम उनका इंतज़ार करें... चुप चाप.

It's best if we just wait for the doctor to return... silently.

Haider is shocked, he angrily gets up and storms out.

68 EXT. DSP'S OFFICE

He comes out and sees Khurram waiting outside at the reception. He looks at him, but doesn't stop. Khurram follows him.

KHURRAM

हैदर... बात सुन मेरी...

Haider... Hear me out...

Haider keeps walking angrily. Khurram catches up with him and grabs Haider's shoulder to turn him around.

KHURRAM

किस से गुस्सा है तू? और किस लिए? वो सिर्फ तेरे बाप नहीं, मेरे इकलौते भाई भी हैं.

Who are you angry with? And why? He's not simply your father... he's my brother as well... my only brother...

Haider looks away. Khurram turns his face around, gently this time.

KHURRAM

15 दिनों में पहली बार मुस्कुराई थी कल तेरी मौजे... रो रो के झेलम बना दी थी उसने घर में... और तू बेशर्म गुस्ताख पूछता है कि हम नाच गा रहे है छुप छुप के...

After weeks, your mother managed a smile. She had been crying herself out for hours. And you accuse us of singing and dancing in joy?

He takes out the newspaper from his pocket, announcing his election candidature.

KHURRAM

ये देख. मैं इलेक्शन लड़ रहा हूँ... किस लिए? पूछ? पूछ?

Take a look. I am running for office. I am contesting the elections. Would you care to know why? Would you?

HAIDER

किस लिए?

Why?

KHURRAM

भाई साहब के लिए और किसके लिए? एक बार मेरे हाथ में पावर आयी तो सारे क़ैदखाने खोद के ढूँढ लाऊँगा उन्हें...

For my brother. Who else! Once I'm in power... I'll search every prison and get him home.

HAIDER

आप इलेक्शन लड़ने का इंतज़ार कीजिए चाचा... मेरी लड़ाई तो शुरू हो चुकी है...

Uncle, you can wait to fight the elections. My fight has already begun.

Khurram watches as Haider walks away while a painful melody kicks in on the soundtrack. A song of 'search' plays in the background.

CUT TO:

69 MONTAGE

70 EXT. VILLAGE STATIONERY STORE - DAY

Haider is at a shop with a photograph of Hilaal. It's the one he found at home - Ghazala has been torn out.

Several cyclostyled copies of the photo are made.

Arshia and Haider paste the copies of the photo on various walls.

CUT TO:

71 EXT. CRPF STATION COMPOUND - DAY

Several people stand in line with photographs of 'disappeared' men, a CRPF officer walks by slowly inspecting the photographs, he is stone-faced. Haider is last in line. The officer stops on seeing Hilaal's photo, he looks at Haider. A beat. He nods in the negative.

CUT TO:

72 INT. JAIL - WAITING ROOM - DAY

Haider stares at the photograph. An old woman sitting beside him sees Hilaal's photo. Their eyes meet, she smiles at him, runs her shrivelled hand over his head and shows him a picture of her young son. They share a sad smile.

He looks up and sees a dozen other people in the same room, with similar photographs of their loved ones. A sudden sense of a reality check hits him.

CUT TO:

73 EXT. ARMY CAMP - DAY

Barbed wire and armed soldiers surround the walls of this impenetrable military camp. Haider walks up to the gate with his rucksack on his back. A couple of jawans standing in a bunker order him to stop. Haider is cold and doesn't respond to their threats. The soldiers warn him again, but as there is no response, they approach him with guns pointed, alarmed. Haider raises his arms as he is pinned to the ground. The soldiers hurriedly search his back; nothing but photocopies of Hilaal's photo pour out.

CUT TO:

74 INT. CRPF CAMP - DAY

Arshia and Haider are inside the cabin of a CRPF officer, going through an album full of photos of men.

CUT TO:

75 EXT. LAKE - DAY

A distraught Haider and Arshia sit on the banks of a lake. They watch some children play on the ice. He is emotionless, just watching them blankly as she gently caresses his hair.

CUT TO:

76 EXT. PAPA-2 INTERROGATION CENTRE-MORNING.

A two-storey white bungalow houses PAPA2 interrogation centre. The windowpanes have black paint on them. Edgy, armed soldiers patrol both sides of the road.

A few dozen distraught, hassled men and women sit on the footpath opposite the building - Haider amongst them. A black army Ambassador car, with heavily-tinted windows, drives towards the gate accompanied by a couple of armed jeeps. The men and women hold framed photographs of their loved ones up in the air.

CUT TO:

77 EXT. RIVERSIDE - DAY

Two men push a long wooden boat into the river. Haider is on board, he has a newspaper in his hand.

HEADLINE: UNIDENTIFIED MAN'S BODY IN SUIT FOUND IN JHELUM

He takes out a copy of Hilaal's photograph. The sun rises over the blue-gray pines and bleached Himalayas circling Srinagar. The boatman stops rowing and takes the picture from Haider. He looks at it carefully, then shakes his head in the negative.

78 EXT. LAWNS - DAY

A group of women is seated on the lawns behind a banner that reads: Association of Parents of Disappeared Persons. It's a quiet demonstration - several photographs are pinned up on a makeshift wall... photographs of disappeared Kashmiri men.

Haider pins up a photo of Hilaal on the wall.

FADE TO:

79 EXT. POLICE MORGUE - DAY

A police truck drives in. The people waiting outside rush in. The paramedics and the policemen take out around a dozen bodies from the truck. Many have their faces blown up, some have limbs missing. They line them up on the morgue verandah on stretchers. Arshia turns her face away, runs towards a corner and vomits. Haider rushes ahead like a mad man, moving from one body to another. On one stretcher a young boy lies drenched in blood. He opens his eyes. Haider screams and steps back.

The boy is alive. He jumps out of the stretcher, looks at everyone and shouts:

DANCING BOY

मियानिहः खोदायो! बह चूस ज़िदे! बह चूस ज़िदे! मैं ज़िंदा हूँ!
मैं ज़िंदा हूँ!

I am Alive!! I am Alive!!

The boy, completely covered in blood, jumps, pumps his arms in the air and laughs and laughs. Then suddenly he runs for the gate and keeps running out of the morgue complex.

CUT TO:

80 INT. SALMAN & SALMAN VIDEO SHOP - DAY

On the TV screen, video footage of Haider and Hilaal. The pleasant memory from the past is played on a VCR inside the dark bedroom. Haider watches it silently, Arshia sitting next to him.

81 INT. SALMAN & SALMAN VIDEO SHOP - DAY

An Ambassador car escorted by a police jeep stops in front of the shop. People anxiously come out of their shops. The Salmans are also uneasy. Khurram steps out of the car. The Salmans get down from their shop and wish him.

82 INT. SALMAN & SALMAN VIDEO SHOP - DAY

Khurram opens the door. Haider covers his eyes from the sunlight. Arshia gets up to greet him.

ARSHIA

सलाम-वाले-कुम चाचा.

Salaam walaikum, uncle.

KHURRAM

वाले-कुम सलाम.

Walaikum salaam.

(to Haider)

दो दिन से फाके पे है तेरी मौजे, कहती है कि जब तक तेरे चाँद से चेहरे का दीदार नहीं हो जाता तब तक पानी का कतरा भी नहीं रखेगी ज़बान पे...

Mister...Your mother hasn't eaten a grain of rice for two days now... She says she won't have a drop to drink unless she sees you.

An irritated look on Haider's face.

83 INT. KHURRAM'S HOUSE - BEDROOM - LATER

Ghazala lies on the bed, her eyes closed. A knock on the door.

KHURRAM

आपके जानिसार-ओ-मुशफाक इश्क़ अंगेज़-ओ लख़्ते जिगर हाज़िर हैं...

Open up Ghazala. I present to you the sparkle of your eyes.... your little prince.

Ghazala smiles through her dry lips.

The door opens. Khurram bows and steps aside. Haider stands there stone-faced. Ghazala smiles and hugs him.

GHAZALA

जाना...

My angel...

CUT TO:

84 INT. KHURRAM'S HOUSE - LIVING ROOM - LATER

On Dastarkhan, Ghazala eats as Haider watches her.

HAIDER

आप दिल्ली जाएंगी ना मौजे...

You know, if you go to Delhi...

तो एक जगह आपकी नौकरी पक्की है...

you will certainly be offered
a job at a place I know...

GHAZALA
कहाँ?
Where?

HAIDER
नेशनल स्कूल ऑफ ड्रामा में.
The National School of Drama.

She smiles mischievously.

HAIDER
ये सलूक बंद कर दें आप अब मेरे साथ...
Please do stop your theatrics now!

GHAZALA
कौन सा सलूक? क्या किया है मैने?
What do you mean? Why am I to blame?

HAIDER

इमोशनल ब्लैकमेल बचपन से छोटी छोटी बातों पे... कभी खाना छोड़ देंगे, तो कभी घर... रोती रहेंगी या मारने की धमकी देंगी...

You always used emotions to manipulate me. Even in my high school... you would stop eating or leave home. You would cry away or threaten suicide.

Ghazala stops eating and looks at him.

HAIDER

ऐसे ही इमोशनल ब्लैकमेल करके आपने मुझे अलीगढ़ भेजा... घर से दूर... ओबुजी से दूर...

That is how you sent me away to Aligarh. Banished me from my home.. Away from home, away from my father...

Ghazala smiles weakly.

GHAZALA

अगर तू अलीगढ़ ना गया होता तो जानता है कहाँ गया होता?

If I hadn't pushed you to Aligarh... you know well where you would have ended up!

They look at each other. A beat.

85 FLASHBACK

Ghazala is in Haider's room cleaning up. She gathers some textbooks to put inside Haider's backpack, and feels a metal thing inside the bag. She pulls it out. It's a pistol. She is shocked.

Haider, age sixteen, being scolded by Ghazala who is freaking out.

GHAZALA

क्या है यह? हाँ? क्या है? किस ने दी ये तुझे?

What is this? Who gave you this?

GHAZALA

जवाब दे?

I demand an answer.

HAIDER

स्कूल में एक दोस्त की है... कल वापस दे दूँगा...

It belongs to a friend. I'll return it tomorrow.

GHAZALA

मिलिटेन्ट्स से दोस्तियाँ बना रहा है तू? आज पिस्टल लाया है... कल कलाशनिकोव लाएगा?

Now you are friends with militants? It is a pistol today, tomorrow it will be a Kalashnikov..

She slaps him hard. Haider is fuming. She holds him by his hair.

GHAZALA

सरहद पार जाएगा तू?

Are you going to cross the border? Going for arms training in Pakistan?

Haider frees himself from her grip and screams.

HAIDER

हाँ जाऊँगा. जाऊँगा सरहद पार...

Yes, I'll go across. I will!

Ghazala is shocked. Tears form in her eyes as Haider leaves to go out. She runs and comes in his way and holds him affectionately.

GHAZALA
जाना... नहीं...
My dear... no...

Haider is quiet. She unties the scarf from her head and puts it on his feet. He steps back. Tears roll off her cheeks.

He suddenly runs out of the house. Ghazala sees him running away into the fields.

CUT TO:

86 INT. KHURRAM'S HOME - DAY

Ghazala rings the bell at the same bungalow which we have seen as Khurram's residence. It has a different name plate, which reads as 'Dr Hussain Meer'.

A young Khurram opens the door. Tears are still rolling off Ghazala's cheeks.

KHURRAM
बाबी-जान... ख़ैरियत तो है?
Are you all right?

She hugs him crying. He slowly puts his arms around her.

CUT TO:

87 INT. KHURRAM'S HOME - LATER

The gun is unwrapped from Ghazala's scarf by an old man, Ghazala's father-in-law Dr Hussain Meer. Ghazala is seated near him, tears in her eyes.

Dr HUSSAIN MEER

हमारा आसमान काले परिंदों से घिरा हुआ है... कहीं किसी चूज़े को चील उठा के ले जाती है तो कहीं बुलबुल को बाज़ ज़िन्दा नोच लेते हैं...

These are dark days. Birds of prey are circling above... They prey without care... Kites grab sparrows and falcons feast on bulbuls..

He takes a deep breath and looks at Ghazala.

Dr HUSSAIN MEER

उसे दूर रखो यहाँ से, मेरा एक दोस्त है अलीगढ़ में, वहाँ पढ़ने भेज दो.

Keep him away from it all. I have a friend at the university in Aligarh... Send him there.

He takes a deep breath.

Dr HUSSAIN MEER

हिन्दुस्तान का दूसरा रूख़ भी देखना ज़रूरी है उसके लिए...

He will get to see the other India.

Dr HUSSAIN MEER

वो हिन्दुस्तान जहाँ न दिन पे पहरे हैं और न रात पे ताले...

A world without imprisoned days
and curfewed nights.

GHAZALA

डॉक्टर साहब कभी तैयार नहीं होंगे...

Doctor Sahib won't let him go.

Dr HUSSAIN MEER

हैं कहाँ तेरे डॉक साहब?

Where is he?

GHAZALA

जम्मु गए हैं कॉन्फ्रेन्स में कल आ जाएंगे.

In Jammu for a conference..

The old man taps her head lovingly.

Dr HUSSAIN MEER

तेरे डॉक्टर साहब का इलाज मैं कर दूँगा. तू हैदर को मना बस... ठीक... अब थोड़ा हँस भी दे मेरी बच्ची... हँस दे.

I'll take care of the doctor. Make Haider come around. Okay? Now cheer up... Smile, my child!

Ghazala giggles through her tears.

Dr HUSSAIN MEER

तेरे इन छन्नाकूँ के बगैर घर बड़ा उदास रहता है...

This house is a ruin without your laughter.

Khurram brings kahwa in a pot and starts putting it into the cups.

GHAZALA

खुर्रम साहेब का निकाह करा दीजिए सब ठीक हो जाएगा...

A bride for Khurram... and it will be a happy home...

Khurram looks at her and smiles. She smiles back.

Dr HUSSAIN MEER
वो मुमकिन नहीं है...
That's impossible...

Khurram hands over the cup of kahwa to Dr Meer.

GHAZALA
(surprised)
क्यों ओबुजी...
Why so?

Dr HUSSAIN MEER
कोई लड़की पसंद ही नहीं आती इसे.
He doesn't seem to like any girl.

Khurram turns and gives the cup to Ghazala.

GHAZALA
क्यों जेनाब खुर्रम?
And why is that, Mister Khurram?

KHURRAM
यूँ बाबी जान कि जितनी भी खूबसूरत लड़कियाँ थीं यहाँ, उन सबके निकाह तो हो चुके हैं... आपकी तरह.
Well! All the pretty ones... are taken... married... just like you!

They hold a look. Khurram suddenly bursts into laughter. Ghazala tries hard to remain normal.

CUT TO:

88 INT. HILAAL'S ROOM IN THE HOSPITAL

Hilaal scribbles a prescription on a piece of paper, as Zahoor and Ikhlaakh look on.

HILAAL

ये कुछ दवाइयाँ है और ये एक इंजेक्शन अभी लगाना पड़ेगा. सामने फार्मेसी है ले आईए.

These medicines... and this injection...
you'll get them at the pharmacy
across the road... please get them.

A knock on the door. Ikhlaakh and Zahoor hold their guns inside their pherans. Hilaal asks them to be calm. He opens the door to find his father standing there.

HILAAL

ओबुजी... आप यहाँ? मुझे बुला लिया होता.

Father... you could've summoned me...
everything ok?

Dr HUSSAIN MEER

अस्पताल की खुशबू भूलने सा लगा था सो चला आया...

I was beginning to forget the smell of the hospital...
so just dropped by...

Dr Hussain enters the room and looks at Ikhlaakh and Zahoor. They wish him gently and get up to leave.

Dr HUSSAIN MEER

अरे कमाण्डर साहब. दो लम्हा... अच्छा हुआ आप मिल गए... कुछ मालूमात करनी थी तुमसे...

Commander Zahoor... Good thing I ran in to
you... needed to ask you something...

ZAHOOR

जी, कहिए?

Yes sir.. ?

Dr HUSSAIN MEER

जेनाब ये... आज़ादी की कोई तारीख़ तय हुई है क्या?

Any date fixed on the independence?

A beat. Suddenly all of them burst into laughter.

CUT TO:

89 EXT. MEDICAL COLLEGE CAMPUS - LATER

Graffiti on the campus walls with slogans like 'Go India Go Back' and 'Hum kya chahte, Aazadi'. Dr Meer and Hilaal walk along the wall.

HILAAL

ओबुजी कौन बाप चाहेगा कि उसका बेटा मिलिटेन्ट बन जाए... लेकिन अपने बच्चों को यहाँ से दूर रखना भी तो इस मर्ज़ का इलाज नहीं है...

No father wants to see his son as a militant... But sending him away is not a way out either...

Dr Meer smiles weakly and looks at Hilaal.

Dr HUSSAIN MEER

बड़ा क़दीम मर्ज़ है बेटा... सदियों पुराना... कितनी नसलें हज़म कर गया है हमारी...

It is a grave problem... and an old one too... We have lost a few generations already...

They reach the parking lot near the car. Dr Meer points at the graffiti on the wall.

Dr HUSSAIN MEER

खुदा जाने कहाँ जा के रूकेगा मौत का ये खूँरेज़ पहिया...
God alone knows when blood will
stop raining on our land...

Zahoor's voice comes from behind.

ZAHOOR

यह तो हिन्दुस्तान के हाथ में है जेनाब...
It's all up to India.

They turn to see Zahoor smiling at them. He hands over the pack of injection he brought from the pharmacy to Hilaal.

ZAHOOR

जैसे वहाँ कहते हैं ना 'जन्मसिद्ध अधिकार'. हम तो बस अपना
अधिकार माँग रहे हैं... आज़ादी...
As they say in India, 'birthright'. And we are only
claiming our right... Freedom.

Dr Meer stops, looks at him and smiles.

Dr HUSSAIN MEER

आज़ादी... हिन्दुस्तान में भी, लाठी वाला लाया था... बंदूक वाला नहीं.
Freedom... The hand that won India its freedom..
did not hold the barrel of a gun. Guns only knows
how to avenge...

Dr Meer puts his hand on Zahoor's shoulder.

Dr HUSSAIN MEER

कमाण्डर साहब... जब तक हम अपने इस इंतक़ाम से आज़ाद नहीं होंगे,
तब तक कोई आज़ादी हमें आज़ाद नहीं कर सकती, याद रखना, इंतक़ाम
से सिर्फ इंतक़ाम पैदा होता है...

Commander... revenge does not set you free...
True freedom lies beyond violence... Remember...
Revenge only begets revenge.

A beat. Dr Meer sits in the car as the driver drives away.

CUT TO:

90 INT. HILAAL'S HOME - DAY

A young Haider screams as Ghazala and Hilaal look on.

HAIDER

बहरे हैं आप लोग? सुनाई नहीं देता? कहीं नहीं जाऊँगा मैं, यहीं रहना है मुझे...

Don't you understand? Can't you hear me? I am not going anywhere. I am staying here.

He looks at Ghazala and whispers.

HAIDER

ओबुजी के पास.

With my father.

Haider storms out of the house. Ghazala looks at Hilaal. They hold a look.

CUT TO:

91 EXT. VILLAGE SQUARE - DAY

A game of cricket at the village square between Haider and his friends. Ghazala emerges out of an alley and walks towards the pitch. Her walk reflects anger. She reaches Haider and faces him. She takes out a pistol from inside the pheran. It's the same pistol she found in Haider's school bag. Haider is stunned. She puts it on her temple.

HAIDER

मौजे... क्या कर रही हैं आप?

What are you doing, mother?!

GHAZALA

आख़िरी बार पूछ रही हूँ... तू जायेगा कि नहीं?

I ask for the last time... Will you go or not?

The villagers gather around them.

HAIDER

मौजे... आप मेरी बात सुनिए... पिस्टल नीचे करिए...

Please listen to me... Please put the gun down, mother...

Ghazala screams aloud as tears roll off her cheeks.

GHAZALA

जायेगा कि नहीं?

Will you go or not?

JUMP CUT TO:

92 EXT. NISHAAT BAGH - DAY

Ghazala and Haider walk amongst fallen chinar leaves, while at a distance commandos guard the road from both ends, holding guns.

HAIDER

उस दिन सच में मार लेती आप गोली?

Would you really have shot yourself that day?

GHAZALA

तुझे शक़ है?

Do you doubt me?

HAIDER

नहीं... यक़ीन है... आप नहीं मारती...

No... I'm sure, you wouldn't have...

She smiles, he smiles back.

GHAZALA

एक बस तू ही मेरे जीने की वजह थी... और है... तेरे जाने के बाद डॉक साहब और मेरे बीच फासले बढ़ते ही गए... सारा साल मैं छुट्टियों में तेरे लौटने के इंतज़ार करती थी और वो ज़ख्मों और बीमारियों में उलझे रहते थे. उनके जिस्म से खून की बू आती थी दिन रात, मौत की बू... इंतज़ार ही तो लिखा है मेरी किस्मत में...

I had little reason to live but for you.. Or was there?
I died everyday. I bore those long, painful years for you... just for your sake. Hilaal had lost himself in the hospital, a saint saving lives. His clothes, his skin reeked of blood. The smell of death.
I had no other reason to live, but you.
I would wait months for you to return home in the holidays. It is my fate to long, to wait...
First for you... Now...

HAIDER

अब क्या करेंगी आप?

And now?

GHAZALA

डिसएपियर्ड लोगों की बीवियों आधी बेवा कहलाती हैं यहाँ... Half-widows.. मैं सिर्फ इंतज़ार कर सकती हूँ...

The wives of disappeared people are called 'half-widows' here. We can only wait.

HAIDER

(smiles sarcastically)

किसका? ओबुजी का?

For father to return?

GHAZALA

हाँ... या फिर उनकी बॉडी का.

Or for his corpse to be returned.

Haider screams.

HAIDER

मेरे ओबुजी ज़िंदा हैं...

My father is alive!

He holds her face in between his palms and shakes violently. She doesn't resist.

HAIDER

समझे, वो ज़िंदा हैं.

He's alive!

He suddenly bursts out crying like a child. He hugs and slides through her neck to bosom to her tummy, on his knees.

He wraps his arms around her waist, buries his face into her stomach and howls.

HAIDER
बोलो ना मौजे... ज़िंदा हैं वो... ज़िंदा हैं...
Please tell me mother, he's alive... He's alive!

FADE TO:

93 EXT. VARIOUS - DAY

We see various parts of Kashmir. The beauty is juxtaposed with the ugly billboards of the various political candidates hanging all over the place.

94 EXT. KASHMIR VILLAGE SQUARE - DAY

We see Zahoor delivering a fiery speech to a small gathering of people.

ZAHOOR

ये डेमोक्रेसी नहीं, धमो-क्रेसी है. इस इलेक्शन का बाइकॉट कर के आप दुनिया को बता दीजिए कि हमारे जख़्मों की शिफ़ा और हमारे दर्द का चारा सिर्फ आज़ादी है... सिर्फ आज़ादी.

It is not a democracy... it's a suffocating system. A suffo-cracy. Freedom... We'll snatch it away... Freedom...

He pauses, looks at the brand new TV by his side with a bullet placed on its top.

ZAHOOR

और कौम के वह गद्दार जो यह इलेक्शन लड़ेंगे, उन्हें गोली के साथ ये कलर टी.वी. मुफ्त मिलेगा.

And the traitor who chooses these sham elections... will get this colour TV and this bullet.

95 EXT. KASHMIR VILLAGE SQUARE - DAY

Khurram delivers a speech with equal gusto to a larger crowd at the spot.

KHURRAM

झण्डे का रंग कोई भी हो, आदमी की जरूरत तो एक ही होती है. हमारे स्कूल आर्मी के कैम्प बन गए हैं और अस्पताल मुर्दा घर.

Wherever you come from...people want the same thing... Our schools have been turned into prisons....

चौराहे बंकरों से घिरे हैं और सड़कें तारून से.

Our town squares are lined with bunkers and streets with barbed wires.

मेरे खुद अपने भाई डिसएपियर्ड हैं महीनों से. अपनों को ढूँढ़ने के लिए हमें ही पुकार लगानी होगी.

My brother disappeared months back. We have to raise our voices to search for our own.

अपने कशमीर की तरक्की के लिए मैं यह गोली का तावीज़ गले में डाल रहा हूँ...

I shall wear this bullet on my neck for the development of Kashmir...

और रात को इस टी.वी. पे इण्डिया-पाकिस्तान का मैच भी देखूँगा.

And watch the India-Pakistan cricket match tonight on this very TV!

CUT TO:

96 INT. KHURRAM'S HOUSE. DAY

Ghazala is watching news on Doordarshan. A newsreader in a sari is talking about polling in Kashmir.

NEWSREADER

आज कशमीर घाटी में आतंकवादी हमले के बीच लोक सभा के चुनाव हो रहे हैं... श्रीनगर, बारामुला और अनन्तनाग में आतंकवादी संगठनों ने तीन विस्फोट किए.

In Kashmir today Lok Sabha elections are being conducted despite militant attacks... Srinagar, Barahmullah and Anantnag witnessed three bombings.

A famous politician surrounded by bodyguards placing his vote.

NEWSREADER

कल दोपहर तक मतगणना पूरी होगी.

Counting shall be completed by tomorrow afternoon.

CUT TO:

97 INT. PARVEZ'S HOME - LIVING ROOM

Arshia listens to the BBC news on a transistor.

NEWSREADER

Elections for local government were concluded in the disputed region of Indian-administered Kashmir today among widespread allegations that thousands of Indian troops coerced reluctant voters into polling booths. India rubbished these allegations.

98 INT. VOTE COUNTING CENTRE - DAY

A heavily-guarded vote-counting centre. Volunteers inside a room tally the handful of votes. Khurram and others are in animated conversation in the background.

NEWSREADER

(off-screen)

However, the voter turnout remained very low. Kashmar constituency saw the lowest turnout, where only 110 votes were registered.

The polling officer comes out and congratulates Khurram.

POLLING OFFICER

(to Khurram)

मुबारक़ हो खुर्रम साहब, आप 100 वोट से जीत गए...

Congratulations! You have won by a hundred votes.

Salman and Salman break out into a huge cheer. Khurram is picked up by some of his supporters on the shoulders. The party workers dance jubilantly and burst fireworks over the beats of a live band.

CUT TO:

99 EXT. CRPF GROUNDS

On stage the members of the Bhaand Pather, traditional folk entertainers of Kashmir, perform in celebration.

Khurram and Ghazala sit on a sofa, amongst other dignitaries of the state like the governor and the army corps commander.

Reporters and cameramen capture their performance. Ghazala beams with happiness and keeps looking stealthily at Khurram from the corner of her eyes.

REPORTER

These traditional folk entertainers, known as the Bhaand Pather, are enacting a play which speaks of a new Kashmir...

a peaceful Kashmir... Will the new regime bring a brighter future for the Kashmiri...? Only time will tell..

The players go on with their performance.

CUT TO:

100 INT. ARMY CAMP - DAY

The corps commander Murthy addresses a group of journalists inside the press room of an army camp.

MURTHY

इलेक्शन पहला क़दम है अमन की दिशा में,
मगर रास्ता अब भी काफी लम्बा है...
Elections are the first step... on the long road to peace... It is a difficult journey... but we can see our destination...

JOURNALIST 1

Associations of Parents of Disappeared People, APDP, के मुताबिक लगभग 8000 लोग अरेस्ट के बाद लापता हैं... your comments...
According to the APDP there are over 8,000 people who are missing since arrest...

MURTHY

Your numbers are wrong. संख्या तो तीन लाख आठ हज़ार होनी चाहिए.
Your numbers are wrong... What about those 300,000 Kashmiri Pandits?

A murmur in the crowd.

MURTHY

जो तीन लाख पंडित अपने घरों से निकल गए और refugee camps में रह रहे हैं, आप उनको disappeared लोगों में नहीं गिनेंगे?

The Pandits who have been displaced from their homes and live as refugees... will you not count them amongst the disappeared?

JOURNALIST

Does the law allow you to use torture on people you arrest?

Murthy looks at the journalist, a bit longer.

MURTHY

The Indian Army is one of the most disciplined armies in the world. We train our officers to interrogate and not torture. मैं आप लोगों को याद दिलाना चाहता हूँ कि जो मुल्क आज गुमराह कशमीरी लड़कों को मासूमों के कत्ल के लिए आर्म्स और training दे रहे हैं, उसी मुल्क के लोगों ने

1948 में क़बालियों के भेस में कशमीरियों को लूटा था... उनकी औरतों को रेप किया था और बच्चों को काटा था. उस वक़्त हिन्दुस्तानी फौज ने ही अपना खून बहाकर हिफाज़त की थी कशमीर की.

The Indian Army is one of the most disciplined armies in the world. We train our officers to interrogate and not torture. I would like to remind you of our neighbour that arms and trains misguided Kashmiri youth to kill innocent people... In 1948, they had looted Kashmiris when they came as tribals... Raped their women and killed their children. It was the Indian Army that shed its blood to save Kashmir.

He pauses for a moment and looks around.

MURTHY

हम नहीं होंगे तो वो फिर वही करेंगे यहाँ... Separatist leaders हिन्दुस्तान से आज़ादी नहीं पाकिस्तान से गुलामी माँग रहे हैं...

And if we aren't around, it'll happen again. Separatists are not demanding freedom from India... but enslavement to Pakistan.

There is silence in the crowd.

MURTHY

Any more questions?

CUT TO:

101 INT. HILAAL'S HOUSE - DAY

Haider sits silently in the damaged area of the house. He has a blank look on his face as he polishes Hilaal's shoes with a brush.

A few snowflakes fall through the broken roof on to him, followed by several more.

FADE OUT.

FADE IN :

102 EXT. VARIOUS - DAY

Kashmir in all its winter glory.

103 EXT. *KASHMIR POST* NEWSPAPER OFFICE

A mysterious man, wearing huge sunglasses and a turban, crosses the road, with the help of a walking stick. An army truck passes him, almost hitting him. He turns around and looks at the truck, then swings his shawl over his shoulders. This is ROOHDAAR, an attractive man in his late forties.

CUT TO:

In a tea shop opposite the newspaper office, Roohdaar reads an issue of Kashmir Post. *The headline reads.*

'Politics Returns, But 8,000 Still Missing in Kashmir' by Arshia Lone.

Arshia's car stops next to the tea shop. She steps out and locks the door.

ROOHDAAR

माशा-अल्लाह...

Nice...

Arshia turns back and looks at him. He waves the newspaper at her. Arshia smiles.

ROOHDAAR

Nice article.

ARSHIA

Thank you.

She moves towards her office building. Next to the staircase of the office, a young boy stands at the entrance of a shop. His old mother is pleading with him to come inside and he is refusing to do so. A crowd has gathered around.

ARSHIA

क्या हुआ इसे?

What's with him?

OLD MOTHER

पता नहीं... आजकल रोज़ दरवाज़े के आगे खड़ा हो जाता है...
घण्टों अंदर नहीं आता.

I don't know... These days he just stands outside the door for hours. He doesn't come in...

Roohdaar's voice comes from behind.

ROOHDAAR

तलाशी लो इसकी...

Search him. Where are you coming from?

Everyone looks back. Roohdaar makes his way through the people, walking with a limp with the support of his walking stick. He faces the boy now.

ROOHDAAR

आई.डी.?

What's in your pockets? ID?

The boy immediately takes out his ID from his pocket. Roohdaar frisks the boy from head to toe.

ROOHDAAR

जाओ.

Go now.

The boy quietly goes inside.

ROOHDAAR

(To Arshia)

तलाशी की इतनी आदत पड़ गयी है यहाँ लोगों की, जब तक कोई टटोल ना ले तब तक अपने घर में भी घुसने की हिम्मत नहीं होती... It's a psychological disorder, called 'New Disease'... डॉक्टर्स इसे नई बीमारी कहते है...

People have become so used to check-posts and body searches at every entrance that unless they are frisked.. they fear crossing a door even to enter their own homes. It's a psychological disorder called 'New Disease'...

Arshia smiles.

ARSHIA

आप doctor हैं?

Are you a doctor?

Roohdaar laughs.

ROOHDAAR

नहीं... doctor की रूह.

A doctor's soul.

Arshia smiles and leaves for the staircase. Roohdaar follows, slowly, limping. She climbs a few steps, stops and turns.

ARSHIA

क्यूँ पीछा कर रहे हैं आप मेरा? क्या चाहते हैं?

Why are you following me? What do you want?

ROOHDAAR

पैग़ाम...

A message...

ARSHIA

वाट?

What?

ROOHDAAR

A message.

Yes, a message.

ARSHIA

मेरे पास किसी के लिए ना कोई message है, ना पैग़ाम.

I have no message to give anyone.

ROOHDAAR

मेरे पास है.... हैदर के लिए उसके ओबुजी का पैग़ाम

But I do... A message for Haider from his father.

Arshia is stunned, she steps down.

ARSHIA

क्या?

What?

Roohdaar smiles.

ROOHDAAR
अब हैदर का पैग़ाम तो हैदर को ही मिलना चाहिए ना, जाना.
A message for Haider shall be delivered
to Haider! Right?

He passes a piece of paper to her.

ROOHDAAR
Phone number है. मैं इंतज़ार करूँगा उसकी आवाज़ का...
Here is my number. I will wait for his call.

A little ahead a column of soldiers is walking closer. Roohdaar slowly turns into a small lane, away from the soldiers. Arshia follows quickly and calls from behind.

ARSHIA
आपका नाम क्या है?
What is your name?

ROOHDAAR
रूह, रूहदार...
Rooh... Roohdaar.

Arshia watches him walk away.

CUT TO:

105 EXT. UN OBSERVER'S OFFICE - SRINAGAR - DAY

Outside the gates of the UN office, the Association of Parents of Disappeared Persons holds a demonstration, with several people, mostly women. They display large banners and photos of disappeared people 'Where is my father?', 'Did they vanish into thin air?' Haider is amongst the crowd, he holds a banner in his hand, it reads:

'Shall we be or not be?' 'हम हैं, कि हम नहीं'

Haider, the Salmans and several others with him shout out the slogan.

ALL

हम हैं, कि हम नहीं?! हम हैं, कि हम नहीं?!

Shall we be, or not be?

Arshia gets out of her car scanning the crowd for Haider. A sense of concern and panic in her actions. She locates him.

ARSHIA

हैदर... हैदर...

Haider...

Haider looks at her but keeps shouting the slogan, aggressively. Salman and Salman look on curiously.

ARSHIA

हैदर... मेरी बात सुनो...

I have to tell you something...

Haider... Listen to me.

She finally holds him and shakes vigorously.

ARSHIA

ओबुजी का message आया है

There's a message from your father.

Haider suddenly stops and looks at Arshia. Salman & Salman get even more curious and alarmed.

CUT TO:

106 INT. PHONE BOOTH - LATER

Inside the booth, Haider dials the number. The phone rings at the other end, nobody answers. Arshia grabs the receiver and listens, still no reply. Disheartened they're about to cut the call when suddenly a hoarse male voice answers the phone. Arshia hurriedly passes the receiver to Haider.

VOICE
हेलो...
Hello..

HAIDER
हेलो...
Hello..

VOICE
कौन?
Who is it?

HAIDER
हैदर
I am Haider...

VOICE
कौन हैदर?
Haider who?

Haider looks at Arshia.

HAIDER
हैदर मीर.
Haider Meer.

VOICE
किससे बात करनी है?
Whom do you want to speak to?

HAIDER
रूह से...
Rooh...

A pause.

VOICE
किसकी रूह से?
Whose Rooh?

Haider looks at Arshia. A beat.

HAIDER
रूहदार...
Roohdaar...

A soft laughter from the other side.

VOICE
Downtown, ज़ैना कदल के पुल पे.... कल सुवह 9 बजे.
Downtown. Zaina Kadal bridge... tomorrow 9 am.

The call is disconnected. Arshia looks at Haider anxiously. The Salmans watch intrigued, trying to figure out the conversation from outside the booth.

CUT TO:

107 EXT. DOWNTOWN SRINAGAR - DAY

Roohdaar stands alone leaning on his walking stick, smoking at the corner of the bridge at Downtown. Across the road, Arshia's car arrives. She recognizes Roohdaar. Their eyes meet, he puts out his cigarette and nods his head backwards, gesturing to be followed. Haider opens the door of the car, Arshia holds his hand.

ARSHIA

Downtown में कुछ भी हो सकता है. Be careful, हैदर.
Anything can happen in Downtown... please be careful, Haider...

Haider presses her hand softly. She hugs him. A photo is clicked. We see Salman and Salman at a distance taking pictures.

Haider gets down and crosses the bridge as Arshia watches him disappear into the alleys.

SALMAN 1
To go?

SALMAN 2
Or not to go?

They look at each other.

CUT TO:

108 EXT. DOWNTOWN SRINAGAR - LANES

Roohdaar marches forward closely followed by Haider. Salman and Salman follow Haider, keeping a safe distance. The lanes get narrower, cold and harsh faces stare at Haider.

Salman and Salman see a few young militants with guns ahead in the street. They are apprehensive, slow down their pace and join a small crowd listening to cricket commentary on radio outside a shop.

The militant boys wish Roohdaar, who nods in return. The militants start to follow Haider.

Salman and Salman walk faster to catch up. Suddenly Salman 2 hears a song coming out of a TV screen from inside a barber shop. He stops and looks at the TV. The song is from a Salman Khan film - 'Kabootar ja ja ja'. *The heroine releases a pigeon from her palms with an envelope around its neck.*

Following Roohdaar, Haider goes deeper into the labyrinth of lanes. As Haider turns a corner, two young men suddenly overpower him and cover his face with a black cloth. He struggles as the men push him into a waiting van at the side.

CUT TO:

108A EXT. ISLAMIC GRAVEYARD - DAY

The same van is parked outside a two-storied house in the middle of the graveyard. A few men unload a large supply of weapons from a car and head inside the house. A couple of teenage boys and a girl help them.

109 INT. ISLAMIC GRAVEYARD

The black hood is raised from Haider's face; he squints as the daylight hits his eyes. Roohdaar sits facing Haider. An old man (gravedigger) places cups of tea in front of them and leaves.

HAIDER
(to Roohdaar)
कहाँ हैं ओबुजी?
Where is my father?

Roohdaar looks at Zahoor.

ZAHOOR
दूर हैं... बहुत दूर...
In a faraway place...

Haider looks back at Roohdaar.

HAIDER
आपने कहा था कि उनका message है मेरे लिए
You said you had a message from him...

ROOHDAAR
है....
Yes.

HAIDER
क्या?
What is it?

Zahoor and Roohdaar look at each other. A beat.

ROOHDAAR
बदला... इंतक़ाम....
Revenge. Vengeance.

HAIDER

किससे इंतक़ाम? किस लिए?

Vengeance. Vengeance from whom? And why?

Roohdaar is quiet.

ZAHOOR

ख़ूनी से... ख़ून के लिए...

To take revenge for a foul and unnatural murder...
by a serpent of a murderer.

Haider turns sharply towards Zahoor. His voice is choking now.

HAIDER

कुछ ग़लतफ़हमी हुई है आप लोगों को.... उन्हें आर्मी ने arrest किया
है... आज नहीं तो कल पता चल जाएगा कि कौन से
कैम्प में रखा है...

You seem to have confused matters... My father
was arrested by the army and one of these days...
we will find out where they hold him.

They stare at him in silence. He gets up hurriedly and walks towards the exit. Roohdaar whispers from behind.

ROOHDAAR

गुलों में रंग भरे बाद-ए-नौ बहार चले.

'Let the petals fill with colour... Let the breeze ruffle
the spring...'

Haider stops. Tears start rolling off his cheeks. Roohdaar walks up to him, turns him around, starts wiping his tears.

ROOHDAAR

चले भी आओ कि गुलशन का कारोबार चले.

'Come along, my love... Awake the garden to life.'

CUT TO:

110 EXT. PAPA-2 INTERROGATION CENTRE - DAY

SUPER: PAPA 2 - DETENTION CENTRE OF THE SECURITY FORCES.

The same two-storey white bungalow. The same black windowpanes. A faint voice softly sings a Faiz Ahmed Faiz poem on the soundtrack.

HILAAL

(voice)

क़फस उदास है यारों सबा से कुछ तो कहो...

The prison is a sullen ghost... Ask the breeze for a whiff of hope ...

111 INT. PAPA-2 INTERROGATION CENTRE - CELLS - NIGHT

A badly-wounded Hilaal sings from inside his cell as shrieks of the other inmates echo through the silent night.

HILAAL

कहीं तो बहरे खुदा आज ज़िक्रे यार चले.

Oh, someone please...

There flows the glory of my beloved...

Roohdaar's voice fades in on the sound track.

ROOHDAAR

(voice-over)

क़ैदखानों में जब सारी चीखें, सारी फ़ुग़ायें गलों में दफ़्न हो जाती थीं, तब एक आवाज़, बिलखते हुए सन्नाटों से सुर मिला के रात के जख़्मों पे मलहम लगाया करती थी.

When fatigue would muffle our screams in the prison… a sole voice would rise through the night.... one voice would echo in the night... a balm to our agony...

We see Roohdaar inside the adjacent cell crowded with twenty-odd men. The floor is bare and smears of blood blemish the whitewashed walls. Every man has a coarse, black blanket for bedding. The blankets are full of lice. The cells are brightly lit.

ROOHDAAR

(voice-over)

रोशनी बुझती नहीं थी कभी ज़िंदों में. बदन के उपर जुएँ रेंगती थी और अंदर अज़गर.

The lights would never be turned off... we craved for the darkness. Lice roamed on our broken bodies and vengeful snakes in our hearts.

Hilaal's beautiful soothing voice goes on reciting the poem on the sound track.

CUT TO:

112 INT. PAPA-2 INTERROGATION CENTRE - TORTURE ROOMS - NIGHT

Different torture rooms and different methods being applied on the captured militants to get out the information.

ROOHDAAR

(voice-over)

जहन्नुम/दोज़ख़ का दूसरा नाम है पापा 2.

Papa-2 was the other name for hell.

इसके अंदर जो जैसा जाता है, वैसा वाहर नहीं आता.

Men returned as shadows of their selves from Papa-2.

Over the above voice-over we see:

A man's hands are tied behind him and a soldier holds him by the hair to make him look directly into a high-voltage bulb. An officer speaks calmly as the prisoner screams.

OFFICER 1

20 मासूम बच्चे मरे तुम्हारे ब्लास्ट में...

Twenty innocent children died in your blasts...

The officer nods at the soldier, who relieves the head. Officer offers him a glass of water.

OFFICER 1

कहाँ छुपे हैं बाकी लोग?

Where are your colleagues hiding?

PRISONER 1

पहाड़गंज... होटल ब्लू स्टार.

Pahargunj... Hotel Blue Star.

A wounded bare-chested prisoner, an officer sits opposite, smokes.

OFFICER

ब्रिगेडियर बादाम से मिले हो कभी?

You must have surely met Brigadier Badaam?

The prisoner is quiet.

OFFICER

अच्छा ये तो पता होगा कि आई.एस.आई. ने उसका नाम ब्रिगेडियर बादाम क्यों रखा?

Do you know why the ISI called him Brigadier Badaam (Almond)?

The prisoner is still quiet.

OFFICER

अफगान वार में शराब नहीं मिलती थी तो उसने बादामों का दूध पीना शुरू कर दिया.

Back in the Afghan war… he ran out of booze and started drinking almond milkshakes…

The officer smiles, the prisoner smiles back. Suddenly the officer stubs the butt on his naked arm. The man screams.

A naked man is tied on a ladder, his pants tied near the ankles. A soldier holds a frightening barking dog by the leash.

PRISONER 2

सर, मैं स्टूडेन्ट हूँ. खुदा की क़सम.

Sir, I swear I'm a student.

दस्तगीर साहब की क़सम, मैं मिलिटेन्ट नहीं हूँ.

I'm not a militant.

A naked man, a chair between his legs. His hand are tied with a rope hanging from the ceiling, his legs are tied to the chair. A camera behind his lower back. A man in plain-clothes sits opposite him.

INTERROGATOR

अनन्तनाग में कितने area commanders हैं तुम्हारी तंज़ीम के?

How many area commanders do you have in Anantnag?

The man is quiet.

INTERROGATOR

निकाह नहीं हुआ ना तेरा?

Do you have any children?

The interrogator nods towards a soldier who is wearing gloves and a mask and holding a copper wire in his hands. He bends down, a suggestion of him picking up his penis and inserting the wire inside. The man screams in pain. The masked soldier nods towards another soldier near the electric board. He puts the switch on. The man shakes violently from the electric current.

113 EXT. OPEN AREA IN PAPA 2 - DAY

A row of soldiers in front of all the prisoners in an open area. Hilaal and Roohdaar stand amongst them. The Indian flag flutters in the morning breeze.

A soldier comes forward.

SOLDIER

सब एक साथ मिलकर बोलेंगे... जय हिन्द.

Let's hear it all together... Victory to India!

Everyone repeats except Hilaal and Roohdaar.

PRISONERS

जय हिन्द.

Victory to India!

SOLDIER

जोर से... जय हिन्द...

Victory to India!

PRISONERS

जय हिन्द.

Victory to India!

An officer notices Roohdaar and Hilaal are not repeating. He points to them. The two are brought out of the line and taken inside.

CUT TO:

114 INT. PAPA-2 INTERROGATION CENTRE - CELLS

Hilaal and Roohdaar being beaten mercilessly inside a room.

ROOHDAAR

(voice-over)

उस दिन के बाद से डॉक साहब और मैं जिस्म-ओ-रूह जैसे हो गए थे.
एक साथ पिटते थे. एक ज़ंजीर में बांधे जाते थे. एक कोठरी में सोते थे.

After that day the doctor and I were always
together... body and soul... We bore our torments
together in the same cell. We were chained
together... tormented together and
put in the same cell.

115 INT. PAPA 2 CELL - LATER

Both are chained, lying inside a brightly-lit cell.

HILAAL

लगता है हम दोनों को मौत भी साथ ही अता करेंगे ये लोग.

It seems we will be killed together as well.

Roohdaar laughs softly.

ROOHDAAR

आप मरेंगे डॉक साहब... मैं नहीं मरने वाला.

You can die, doctor, but I won't.

Hilaal is amused.

HILAAL

कैसे जनाब?

And how is that?

ROOHDAAR

ऐसे कि मैं रूह हूँ. और आप जिस्म. आप फानी... मैं लफानी.

Because you are the body and I'm the soul... You are mortal and I'm immortal!

Both share a laugh.

HILAAL

रूहदार तुम शिया हो या सुन्नी?
Are you a Shia or a Sunni?

Roohdaar smiles.

ROOHDAAR

दरिया भी मैं... दरख़्त भी मैं... झेलम भी मैं चिनार भी
मैं दैर हूँ... हराम भ्री हूँ... शिया भी हूँ...
सुन्नी भी हूँ... मैं हूँ पंडित... मैं था मैं हूँ और मैं ही रहूँगा...
वर्ना कौन सुनाएगा यह सच्ची कहानियाँ वक़्त को...
I am the river and the tree... The Jhelum and the chinar... Fortitude and forbidden... A Shia and a Sunni, I'm both... A Pandit as well... I always was... I am... I will always be... Who else will etch these stories in the pages of history...

CUT TO:

116 INT. ARMY TRUCK - DAY

Roohdaar, Hilaal and half a dozen other detainees sit in the back of the truck. It's pitch black.

ROOHDAAR

(voice-over)

फिर हमें interrogations के लिए दूसरे कैम्पों में भेजा जाने लगा...
नए कैम्प्स अनोखे नामों वाले - गो गो लैण्ड, कार्गो, होटल 4.
They moved us to other camps for interrogation. Strange camps... stranger names.... Gogoland, Cargo... Shiraz cinema...

Suddenly the cover is raised and bright sunlight shines onto their eyes. They cover their eyes with their hands. Hilaal and the others are paraded into the building, forced by their chains to take small steps.

ROOHDAAR

फिर एक दिन शायद, गोगो लैण्ड ही था, हम पर सारे राज खुल गए.

And one day, there was a revelation.

ROOHDAAR

किसने दग़ा की थी और कौन गद्दार था, पता चल गया. डॉक साहब की बीवी के अलावा किसी और को पता नहीं था उस खुफिया कमरे के बारे में, जहाँ उस रोज इख्लाख़ छुपा था.

It was Khurram who betrayed your father. The army crackdown in your village was not a matter of chance. And Ghazala had informed Khurram.

As they walk, Hilaal sees something at a distance. A face he can never forget. Khurram in lawyer's attire, shaking hands with a man in an army uniform as he gets into a car. For what seems to be a split second, the brothers' eyes meet.

ROOHDAAR

गज़ाला ने दगा की और खुर्रम ने गद्दारी. उन दोनों का मियाँ-बीवी की तरह साथ रहना इस बात का सबूत है.

Ghazala deceived your father and Khurram betrayed him. That they live like a married couple is proof of that.

FLASH CUT TO:

117 INT. VARIOUS JAILS - DAY

Khurram meets an arrested militant in jail. The militant signs his vakalatnama. Khurram meets several other militants in prison, getting more signatures.

ROOHDAAR

कशमीर में पकड़े गए और सरेंडर हुए मिलिटेन्ट्स के सब से ज्यादा
केसेज़ खुर्रम के पास थे...

Khurram had handled most of the cases of militants
caught or surrendered in Kashmir.

118 I/E. COURT - DAY

The same militants being produced in court, getting bail, boarding awaiting police vehicles.

ROOHDAAR

इखवाँ-उल-मुसलमीन फोर्स को बनाने में खुर्रम ने,
फौज का साथ दिया...

He worked with the Indian intelligence...
to form a militia that would kill
their own people...

119 EXT. ARMY CAMP - DAY

The vehicles enter the camp, the militants alight. Inside, they're given black combat uniforms, ID cards, weapons, bulletproof vehicles etc,.

ROOHDAAR

इखवाँनियों को मिलिटेन्ट्स के हमदर्द और काम
करने के ढ़ंग दोनों पता थे...

Ikhwaan-ul-Muslimeen. The Ikhwaans were our
own. Kashmiris! They knew the militants - the
sympathizers, the operational details..

Khurram, Parvez and Brig Murthy watch proudly as the Ikhwaan-ul-Musalmeen is born.

120 I/E. VARIOUS

A quick montage of Ikhwaanis and their brutality.

- empty bullet shells fly out of guns, grenades and mines explode.

- crying women and children.

- Ikhwaans drag a couple of men out of a hidden wall.

- village houses engulfed in flames.

- Ikhwaans walk proudly with AK 47s over their shoulders.

- Bodies of slaughtered young men displayed proudly by Khurram at an army camp .

- Juxtaposed with visuals of splattered blood and newspaper headlines of Ikhwaan brutality.

121 INT. PAPA-2 INTERROGATION CENTRE - CELLS - NIGHT

Hilaal hums a Faiz poem softly as Roohdaar listens with his eyes closed.

HILAAL

हम देखेंगे... लाज़िम है कि हम भी देखेंगे....

It is certain. We shall witness...The promised day...
the day of the blessed word...We shall witness...

After a few lines he stops and looks at Roohdaar.

HILAAL

रूहदार... अगर तुम वाक़ई में बच गए तो मेरा एक पैग़ाम देना.

Roohdaar... If you do make it out alive... carry a message for me.

Roohdaar turns.

ROOHDAAR

किसे?

To whom?

HILAAL

मेरे बेटे हैदर को. उससे कहना कि मेरा इंतक़ाम ले... मेरे भाई से.

To my son, Haider. Tell him to avenge my betrayal by my serpent of a brother.

Hilaal's eyes are filling up with tears of vengeance.

HILAAL

उसकी उन दो आँखों में गोलियाँ दागे, जिन आँखों से उसने उसकी माँ पर फरेब डाले थे. वो दो आँखें जो उसे यतीम बना गए हैं...

Tell him to aim his bullets at those cunning, deceiving eyes... that entrapped his mother... that made him an orphan.

ROOHDAAR

और माँ?

And his mother?

Hilaal smiles sarcastically.

HILAAL

उसे अल्लाह से इंसाफ के लिए छोड़ दे... वो ज़िंदा रहे ताकि हर आती जाती सांस में उसका ज़मीर उसे कचोटे, नोचे... ज़िंदगी मौत से भी बदतर हो जाए उसकी...

God will be her judge...

A solider knocks at the cell.

SOLDIER

उठो... जिस्म-ओ-रूह... चलो...

Move it, body and soul!

He starts to unlock the cell. Hilaal and Roohdaar look at each other.

ROOHDAAR

(voice-over)

Security forces के लिए हम लोग अब बोझ बन गए थे... इसलिए उन्होंने हमें इख़ानियों को सौंप दिया

We were a burden for the security forces.
They handed us over to the Ikhwaan.

CUT TO:

122 EXT. ZERO BRIDGE - NIGHT

Midnight. The Jhelum flows rapidly underneath. Ikhwaani vehicles flank the bridge from both ends. Roohdaar and

Hilaal are pulled out from the back of the jeep by Ikhwaan soldiers.

Ikhwaanis show them the way with the help of a flashlight, pushing them forward. A flash of light falls onto the passenger seat of a jeep for a brief moment. Enough for Hilaal to see Khurram watching them coldly. A beat.

The Ikhwaanis poke them with their guns, urging them on. Hilaal and Roohdaar walk confidently and defiantly, aware of their impending fate.

An Ikhwaani opens fire on Hilaal. He is down in seconds. Roohdaar tries to scream but nothing comes out of his throat. He is immediately shot on the chest. They tie Hilaal's dead body to Roohdaar's. From the corner of the bridge, both bodies are thrown into the river. The speedy current carries both the bodies away.

ROOHDAAR

फिर दिखाया मेरे परवरदिगार ने मौजज़ो... जिस रस्सी से हमें बांधा था वो खुद ब खुद खुल गया. झेलम का सर्द पानी दवा बन गया. मेरे रिस्ते जख़्मों का खून सोख गया.

It was a miracle! The rope that bound us came loose...The icy water of the Jhelum stopped my bleeding.

CUT TO:

123 I/E. ISLAMIC GRAVEYARD - NIGHT

They sit on the terrace. Roohdaar speaks as Haider sits emotionless. Zahoor watches silently.

ROOHDAAR

झेलम किनारे रेत निकालने वालों ने मेरा इलाज कराया. फिर कुछ दिन बाद उन्होंने डॉक्टर साएब की वॉडी भी ढूँढ़ निकाली.

Some villagers who were sandmining on the river bank saved me. A few days later, they found the doctor's body.

A beat. Zahoor comes to Haider and caresses his hair tenderly.

ZAHOOR

बारामुल्ला के आगे बोनियर गाँव में एक कब्रिस्तान है जहाँ अंजान, बेशिनाख्त शहीदों को दफ़न किया जाता हैं.

A little ahead of Baramulla, at Boniyar village there is a graveyard... where the unknown dead are buried.

Haider is still. No sign of any emotion in his eyes.

ROOHDAAR

डॉक्टर साहेब वहीं दफ़न है. 318 नम्बर क़ब्र में.

They took the doctor's body there. He rests in grave number 318.

Zahoor brings out a small Chinese pistol and puts it on his palm. He shows a small pin at the butt.

ZAHOOR

ये safety lock है. करीब से मारना.

This is the safety lock. Shoot him at point blank.

Roohdaar turns Haider by the chin to face him.

और याद रहे... उन दो आँखों में, जिनसे उसने तुम्हारी मौजे पर फरेब
डाले हैं. वो आँखें जो तुम्हें यतीम बना गई.

And remember... aim at the eyes
that entrapped your mother... Those treacherous
eyes that orphaned you.

Haider looks at the pistol blankly.

CUT TO:

124 INT. SHAH-E-HAMDAN SHRINE - NIGHT

The shrine on the top of a mountain is an old, ornate, wooden shrine, painted green. Haider lies in an inner area of the shrine, the hamaam, where it is warm. His eyes are wide open and blank.

125 I/E. SHAH-E-HAMDAN SHRINE - DAY

A chorus of bhajan-style Kashmiri prayer: Old men shaking their heads, their voices rising up and down, reaching a crescendo. Haider sits in one corner with his eyes closed.

126 EXT. NUMBERED GRAVEYARD - DAY

Haider stands in front of the numbered graveyard. Innumerable graves with a number carved on the epitaph of the each grave.

CUT TO:

127 INT. NUMBERED GRAVEYARD OFFICE - DAY

An old man, the caretaker, flips through a photo album. Each photograph of the dead body has a number. He reaches the number 318. It's Hilaal's disfigured body indeed. Haider looks at the picture.

128 EXT. NUMBERED GRAVEYARD - GRAVE NO 318 - DAY

Grave no 318. Haider cries uncontrollably while sitting on his haunches.

CUT TO:

129 EXT. ZERO BRIDGE - NIGHT

Haider stands looking down at the silent flowing water. Tears rolling off his cheeks.

A looney smile emerges on his lips.

He suddenly jumps into the water.

JUMP CUT TO:

130 INT. KHURRAM'S HOUSE BEDROOM - DAY

Ghazala wakes up with a start. Morning sunlight is coming through the curtains of the windows. She looks at Khurram sleeping next to her on the bed.

CUT TO:

131 INT. KHURRAM'S HOUSE LIVING ROOM - LATER

Ghazala listens to a bell ringing on the receiver of a telephone. Khurram's voice comes from behind.

KHURRAM

किसे अज़ान दे रहीं हैं आप सबह सुबह?

Who are you calling so early in the morning?

She looks at him standing at the door of the bedroom. She puts the receiver down. Khurram comes and sits behind her.

GHAZALA

रात बहुत बुरा ख्वाब देखा.

I had a scary dream.

Khurram embraces her from behind.

KHURRAM

किसका?

What was it about?

Ghazala is quiet.

KHURRAM

हैदर का?

Haider?

Ghazala turns to look at him.

GHAZALA

दो दिन हो गए उसका कुछ पता नहीं. ना अर्शी को, ना सलमानों को.

It's been two days, there's been no word of him.
Neither Arshee nor the Salmans...

KHURRAM

दरगाह पे होगा... आजकल वहीं सोया करता है वो.

Must be at the mosque... I've heard he spends his nights there...

GHAZALA

मैं गई थी दरगाह... पर वहाँ भी इसकी कोई खबर नही है.

I went there too... no sign of him.

He turns her face around.

KHURRAM

अब बच्चा नहीं है वह... आ जाएगा वापस.

My dearest... He's not a child anymore. He'll be back.

Khurram brushes her hair gently.

KHURRAM

कल स्कूल के प्रिंसिपल मिले थे. पूछ रहे थे कि आप स्कूल जाना कब शुरू करेंगी?

I bumped into the principal of your school yesterday. He wanted to know when you are returning to teach... The children miss you very much...

GHAZALA

एक बार पूरी हो जाऊँ... तब.

After this life between places is over.

KHURRAM

(amused)

अभी क्या हैं आप? आधी?

What do you mean?

Ghazala nods.

GHAZALA

जी. आधी बेवा हूँ और आधी दुल्हन.

I am partly a widow and partly a bride.

Khurram taps her head affectionately.

KHURRAM

आधी पागल भी हैं आप... जान...

You are partly a fool as well.

She hugs him tight and closes her eyes.

CUT TO:

132 INT. KHURRAM'S OFFICE IN SECRETARIAT - DAY

Khurram sits opposite as Parvez goes through the photographs of Haider at Downtown bridge. Salman and Salman on either side of the table. A back shot of Roohdaar. Parvez is alarmed, he quickly flips through other photographs and stops on one in which Roohdaar can clearly be seen.

PARVEZ

(whispers)

रूहदार...

Roohdaar!

Khurram takes the picture from him and looks at it. His eyes meet with Parvez's. A beat. Salman brings out an electronic receipt of the PCO.

SALMAN 2

ये वो नम्बर है जिस पर उन्होंने फोन किया था. Satellite नम्बर मालूम पड़ता है... Trace नहीं हो पाएगा...

This is the number he called. It is a satellite phone..
It can't be traced.

Parvez turns to Salmaans.

PARVEZ

पता?

Directions?

The Salmaans look at each other.

SALMAAN 1

लापता...

Directionless...

PARVEZ

मतलब?

Meaning?

He fumbles.

SALMAAN 2

जी लापता हो गए...

We lost them after a point, sir...

PARVEZ

कैसे?

How?

SALMAN 1

जी... वो बस चुटज़्पा हो गया

Sir... chutzpah...

PARVEZ

क्या?

What?

SALMAN 2

ज़हूर का इलाक़ा था जेनाब... अचानक एक गली में मुड़े कि सामने ढ़ेर सारे लड़के. उनके हाथों में कलाशनिकोफ और हमारे हाथों में कैमरा... मतलब चुटज़्पा.

It was Zahoor's stronghold... everywhere you looked, there were dozens of guys with Kalashnikovs... the only weapon we had was our camera...

SALMAAN 1

बाल बाल बच गए सर वर्ना वहीं कर्ण-अर्जुन हो गया था हमारा...

Barely made it out... or else we'd be mincemeat...

Parvez looks at the next photograph. It's Arshia hugging Haider in the car before he leaves.

SALMAN 1

How sweet!

Parvez looks at him sharply, he fumbles.

SALMAAN 1

Sorry... जेनाब...

Sorry, sir...

Salmaan 2 hits Salman 1 angrily and turns to Parvez.

SALMAAN 2

जेनाब वो... नौकरी permanent करने की बात की थी आपने...

Sir, you had mentioned a permanent job for us.

Parvez gestures to them to sign off. Both of them leave. Parvez turns to Khurram and points at Haider in the photograph.

PARVEZ

इसकी रूखसती का वक़्त आ गया है.

It's time to end this...

He looks at Khurram for approval. Khurram is silent. A beat.

KHURRAM

नहीं...

No...

PARVEZ

(surprised)

क्यों?

Why?

KHURRAM

बहुत प्यार करता हूँ मैं.

I can't do that to someone I love..

PARVEZ

(amused)

इस हरामज़ादे से?

You love this brat?

Khurram looks away.

KHURRAM

इस हरामज़ादे की माँ से.

The brat's mother...

PARVEZ

मगर जेनाब आप...

But...

Khurram cuts him in the middle.

KHURRAM

ज़हूर का क्या price देगी आर्मी आपको अंदाज़ है...

What's the reward on Zahoor's head?

Parvez's eyes light up.

KHURRAM

ज़हूर तक पहुँचने का रास्ता है, हैदर.

We can get to him via Haider...

KHURRAM

अब वो ख़तरा भी है आपके लिए.

In fact he's more a threat to you now.

Khurram smiles, picks up a photograph and shows him.

KHURRAM

मुझसे ज्यादा आपकी जान को...

More than ever to your loved ones...

Parvez looks at the photograph of Arshia hugging Haider.

CUT TO:

133 INT. GIFT SHOP - DAY

A small board on the cash counter announces: '1 Rupee per call (for 3 minutes only)'. Arshia holds the receiver and listens to the ring on the other side. Roohdaar's chit with a phone number scribbled over it lying next to the phone.

The salesman comes and hands her a packet wrapped in bright gift paper.

The phone keeps ringing on the other side. Dejected, she puts it down and looks at the gift-wrapped packet, picks up the chit and leaves.

CUT TO:

134 INT. PARVEZ HOME - DAY

Parvez cooks in the kitchen as the servants help. Arshia comes from behind, her bag still slung on her shoulder. She puts the gift-wrapped packet in front of his eyes.

ARSHIA
Surprise.

Parvez turns holding the marinated meat balls in his hands.

PARVEZ
क्या है इसमें?
What is that?

ARSHIA
खोल के देखिए.
Surprise.

Parvez shows her the hands soaked in the batter.

PARVEZ

खोल ना.

Oh… let's open it…

She opens the packet and out comes the red woollen muffler she had been knitting for him. She wraps it around his neck. He is overwhelmed by emotions, pulls her nose.

PARVEZ

कब पूरा किया तूने.

When did you weave it?

The batter covers her nose, she hugs him. Later, both of them eat, sitting on the floor. Parvez serves her.

PARVEZ

थोड़ा गोश्त और लो. कितनी मेहनत से पकाया है मैंने… तुम्हारे लिए.

Here, have one more. It took a lot to make this for you.

ARSHIA

नहीं डैडी. भूख नहीं है.

No daddy. I'm not hungry.

Parvez casually whispers while eating.

PARVEZ

खाना पीना छोड़ने से जल्दी वापस नहीं आने वाला वह.

He is not going to return sooner if you stop eating.

Arshia is stunned. She looks at him, he is still busy in his food.

PARVEZ

कौन लाया था उसके लिए पैग़ाम?

Who brought him the message?

She is quiet. He looks at her.

PARVEZ

रूहदार?

Roohdaar?

Arshia looks down. He makes a bite for her.

PARVEZ

मुँह खोलो...

Open your mouth.

Tears are forming in her eyes. She opens her mouth.

PARVEZ

हैदर का ख्याल रखना होगा... हम सबको मिलकर.
आगे से कुछ छुपाना मत मुझसे...

We'll have to watch out for Haider... Together.
Please don't hide anything from me.

He feeds her the bite.

CUT TO:

135 I/E. AISHMUQAM SHRINE - DAY

Ghazala ties a thread and prays. She takes the maulvi's blessings and leaves.

CUT TO:

136 EXT. SRINAGAR STREETS - LATER

Khurram and Ghazala travel in the car. She looks out of the window, expressionless. Khurram puts his hand on her shoulder.

CUT TO:

137 EXT. LAL CHOWK - SRINAGAR - LATER

Khurram's car takes a turn onto a street where there is a traffic jam. The driver curses in Kashmiri. Khurram looks up front.

KHURRAM

क्या हुआ...?

What's happened?

DRIVER

(in Kashmiri)

पता नहीं साहब.

Traffic is blocked at the square...

He hurriedly steps out of the car to see the extent of the jam. He looks through the various vehicles standing in front.

Through the vehicles and crowd the cause of the jam is revealed. It's Haider! With a clean-shaven head and beard he stands in the middle of the main square, wearing the American flag as a bandana around his forehead on an old suit slightly large for him. He has a stethoscope around his neck like a tie. A transistor radio-cassette player is tied to his back, speakers outwards, its antenna pulled all the way out. He has a glint in his eyes, a touch of instability.

It takes Khurram a moment to recognize him. Ghazala also comes out. She is shocked to see Haider in this new avatar.

He begins to orate loudly as if giving a speech, but to nobody in particular.

HAIDER

UN Council resolution number 47 of 1948,
Article 2 of the Geneva convention and
Article 370 of the Indian Constitution बस एक सवाल उठाते हैं... सिर्फ़ एक... हम हैं कि हम नहीं? हम हैं तो क्यों हैं और नहीं हैं तो कहाँ गए... क्यों हैं तो किस लिए और कहाँ गए तो कब? जेनाब... हम थे भी की हम थे ही नहीं? चुटज़्पा हो गया हमारे साथ. चुटज़्पा पता है आप लोगों को?

Hello... Hello... mic testing one, two, three... Can you hear me? Hello... According to the UN council resolution number 47 of 1948... Article 2 of the Geneva convention and article 370 of the Indian Constitution... There is but one question! Do we exist or do we not? If we do... then who are we? If we don't... then where are we? If we exist, then why do stand here? If we don't exist, where did we lose ourselves? Did we exist at all? or not? Our suffering comes from their chutzpah.

He looks around. People are quiet.

HAIDER

एक बार एक बैंक में डकैती हुई... डाकू ने कैशियर के सिर पे पिस्टल रखी और बोला पैसा दे वर्ना मौत ले... कैशियर ने झट से सारे रूपए निकाले और उसे थमा दिए... डाकू वो पैसा ले के नेक्स्ट काउन्टर पे गया और बोला 'एक फॉर्म दे, एकाउन्ट खोलना है मुझे'.

Once upon a time a bank was robbed. The burglar held a gun and demanded... Give me all the money... or I'll kill you.The cashier gave him all the money. He went to the next counter... And asked the man to open an account for him.

People burst into laughter.

HAIDER

ये होता है चुटज़पा... बेशर्म, गुस्ताख जैसे अफ़्स्पा... अफ़्स्पा...
That is chutzpah... Such audacity, such stupidity...
like AFSPA...

He takes a deep breath and blurts out rapidly in one breath.

HAIDER

Armed Forces Special Powers Act, section 5, rule 4, point A. Any commissioned officer, warrant officer, non-commissioned officer or any other person of equivalent rank in the armed forces may, in a disturbed area, (a) if he is of opinion that it is necessary to do so for the maintenance of public order, after giving such due warning as he may consider necessary, fire upon or otherwise use force, even to the causing of death, against any person who is acting in contravention of any law or order.

He stops to breathe.

HAIDER

लॉ... आर्डर...
Law... Order...

He starts clapping to create a rhythm. People join him. He starts jumping. Tears are streaming off Ghazala's eyes. She can't take it anymore. She walks back to her car. Khurram looks at her walking away.

HAIDER

(on an up tempo beat of claps)

लॉ एण्ड आर्डर लॉ एण्ड आर्डर... आर्डर आर्डर, लॉ एण्ड आर्डर. ना

लॉ है और ना है आर्डर. जिसका लॉ है उसका आर्डर... Made on order Law and Order... इण्डिया पाकिस्तान ने मिलकर खेला हमसे बार्डर बार्डर, आर्डर आर्डर, लॉ एण्ड आर्डर. ना अब छोड़े हमे हिन्दुस्तान ना अब छोड़े हमे पाकिस्तान... पर कोई तो हमसे भी पूछो... कि हम क्या चाहते?

Law and order... Order order... Law and order... There is no law, there is no order. Whose laws? Whose order? Made on order... Law and order... India! Pakistan! A game on the border. India clings to us... so does Pakistan... What of us? What do we want?

A beat. Suddenly the whole crowd screams.

CROWD

आज़ादी.

Freedom!

Khurram moves ahead towards Haider, followed by his commandos. Haider gestures like a traffic policeman. Stretching his arms to right and left.

HAIDER

इस पार भी लेंगे आज़ादी... उस पार भी लेंगे आज़ादी... हम ले के रहेंगे आज़ादी...

Freedom from this side... Freedom from that side...

Khurram climbs up on the traffic platform.

KHURRAM

हैदर!

Haider!

Haider turns back to see Khurram surrounded by commandos. He straightens up and pushes the play button of his cassette player and starts singing along.

HAIDER

सारे जहाँ से अच्छा हिन्दुस्तान हमारा...

'A world better than the world, our India. We are her children...'

Khurram shakes him violently.

KHURRAM

हैदर...

Haider...

Haider stops and looks at him.

KHURRAM

(whispers)

मौजे...

Mother...

CUT TO:

138 EXT. KHURRAM'S CAR AT LAL CHOWK

Haider comes to the car and stands in front of the window.

HAIDER

अरे मौजे आप कब आयीं?

When did you come?

Ghazala looks at him, her face drowned in tears.

HAIDER

आप रो क्यूँ रही हैं? खुशखबरी है आपके लिए, अब आप आधी बेवा नहीं रहीं. ओबुजी मर गए. He's dead. बॉडी भी ढूँढ़ ली है मैंने.

Why are you crying? There's good news for you. Nobody will call you a half-widow now... Father is dead. He is dead. I found his grave.

He moves closer and whispers.

HAIDER

अब आप दोनों को छुप-छुप कर duet गाने की ज़रूरत नहीं है...

You are free of your secret.

She is shocked... looks at Khurram.

HAIDER

यकीन नहीं आता ना आपको. एक मिनट.

You don't believe me, right?

He looks for something in the pockets of his suit and finally finds the photograph of Hilaal's disfigured body.

HAIDER

ये देखिए...

I have a photograph.. my dead father...

She looks at the photograph and goes numb. Khurram takes the photograph from her hands and looks at it too. As Haider raises his eyebrows to tease them.

CUT TO:

139 EXT. NUMBERED GRAVEYARD - DAY

A Muslim priest recites 'fateha' at the grave of Hilaal, which now has a carved epitaph. Khurram, Parvez and many others have their hands raised in prayer for the peace of the dead soul.

Faraway, Haider, still dressed in the same suit, plays cricket with young kids.

CUT TO:

140 EXT. KHURRAM'S HOUSE - DAY

The preparation for the 'choorim' (chautha) mourning ceremony at home. Kahwa is being served to the guests.

CUT TO:

140A INT. BEDROOM IN KHURRAM'S HOUSE

Haider holds the Chinese pistol Zahoor had given him. His face is cold but his eyes rage with fury. A knock on the door. He puts the gun back into his rucksack.

CUT TO:

140B EXT. BEDROOM IN KHURRAM'S HOUSE

Haider opens the door to find Khurram standing at the door. They keep staring at each other. Khurram slowly brings a file up, it has the emblem of the Indian Army and a red label announcing 'Confidential'.

Inside:

Khurram opens the file on a small table as Haider looks on.

KHURRAM

भाई साहब को तो नहीं ढूँढ़ पाया मैं...

I couldn't find my brother.

He looks at Haider, his voice trembling.

KHURRAM

लेकिन उनका क़ातिल जरूर ढूँढ़ लिया है.

But I have found his killer.

He picks a photograph and holds it for Haider. It's Roohdaar, looking totally different. Haider is shocked.

KHURRAM

पापा 2 में भाई साहब का cell mate...

आजकल इसका नाम रूहदार है.

He shared his cell at Papa-2.
He goes by the name Roohdaar...

Haider looks at him questioningly.

KHURRAM

हम... आजकल... इसका असली नाम किसी को नहीं पता. इसकी हर आइडेंटिटी घोस्ट आइडेंटिटी है, झूठी. '90 में पाकिस्तान से आया था. आई.एस.आई. एजेन्ट...

No one knows his real name. Every identity of his is fake. He came from Pakistan in 1991.
An ISI agent.

He shows more photographs of him with men in Pakistani army uniforms.

KHURRAM

2 साल पहले बारामुल्ला में पकड़ा गया. फिर इसने इण्डियन आर्मी के साथ सौदा किया.

Two years back, he was arrested in Baramulla. He cut a deal with the Indian Army...

He shows more papers.

KHURRAM

और डबल एजेन्ट बनकर ज़हूर के ग्रूप में जाकर मिल गया. उसका ये सच भाई साहब को पता था इसलिए उसने अपने साथ भाई साहब की रिहाई भी करायी, और रास्ते में उन्हें मार कर झेलम में...

He penetrated Zahoor's group... A double agent... Brother knew of this fact about him. Which is why he negotiated... brother's release as well. On the way out... he... killed him... and pushed him into the Jhelum river...

His eyes are filled with tears, he wipes them and picks another photograph of Zahoor and Roohdaar.

KHURRAM

इन लोगों ने मारा है मेरे भाई को.

These people have killed my brother.

He holds Haider's hand and speaks in a choked voice.

KHURRAM

वादा करता हूँ कि जब तक मैं इनके खून में नहीं नहा लेता तब तक चैन से नहीं बैठूँगा.

I promise that I will not rest... until I have avenged my brother. I promise...

Just then Arshia enters the room.

ARSHIA

हैदर.

Haider.

She stops seeing Khurram in an emotional state. Khurram smiles.

KHURRAM

आओ princess... आओ.

Come in, little princess...

He quickly picks up the file and leaves. Arshia comes close to Haider, she looks quite angry.

ARSHIA

कितने काहिल इन्सान हो यार तुम. पहले तो इतने दिन गायब रहे और फिर वापस आकर खबर भी नहीं की.

What an imbecile you are!! You disappear for days! And you won't even check on me when you are back!

Haider is quiet, still lost in Khurram's episode. She shakes him violently.

ARSHIA

मैं बेफिज़ूल ही मरती रही तुम्हारी फिक्र में... हाँ...?

I worry for you in vain...

Haider looks at her and smiles weakly.

ARSHIA

ये क्या हाल बना रखा है अपना?

You are so haggard. You've become weak...

Haider hugs her.

HAIDER

तो पूछो ना कि कुछ लेते क्यों नहीं...

Why don't you find me a cure!

Arshia slaps his back again and again and in mock anger.

CUT TO:

140C INT. KHURRAM'S HOUSE - DAY

The ceremony has begun inside. Khurram reads the verse along with the priest, while Ghazala counts chickpeas in an earthen pot full of water. Arshia sits with Haider at the back of the room, in changed clothes. Parvez and others sit silently in prayer.

The ceremony comes to an end. Khurram gets up from his seat and addresses the crowd.

KHURRAM

हमारे ग़म में शामिल हो कर हमारा दर्द बाँटने के लिए आप लोगों का बहुत शुक्रिया... भाई साहब की जुदाई का दर्द तो दिल ने किसी तरह बर्दाश्त कर लिया... पर बाबी-जान को ता उम्र बेवा और हैदर को यतीम देखने की ताकत अब कहाँ से लाऊँ मैं...

Thank you for being with us in this time of grief. Somehow, I have managed to embrace this loss... but... the prospect of seeing my beloved sister-in-law live a widow's life... and my dearest Haider as an orphan... How will I find the courage to bear with that?

A beat.

KHURRAM

इसलिए आप सब बुज़ुर्गों और दोस्तों की मौजूदगी में, मैं अपनी बाबी जान गज़ाला से निकाह की इजाज़त चाहता हूँ.

And thus facing these facts, I seek your permission... the elders and friends here... to marry my sister-in-law Ghazala Meer...

A beat, the crowd is silent. Parvez smiles.

PARVEZ

अल्हम दुल इल्लाह...

Congratulations!

Salman and Salman take the cue and whispers loudly and prompt the guests.

SALMAANS

अल्हम दुल इल्लाह... मुबारक!!

Congratulations!

Suddenly all the guests murmur.

ALL

अल्हम दुल इल्लाह... मुबारक!!!

Congratulations! Congratulations!

Ghazala has a timid smile on her face. Haider's jaws tighten as he looks at his mother's smiling face through the crowd. Khurram looks at Haider and smiles. Haider's eyes display hatred and hurt. Khurram's smile fades out. Ghazala follows Khurram's gaze, Haider is gone.

CUT TO:

141 EXT. BHAAND VILLAGE - DAY

A group of street theatre actors rehearse the dance in the middle of the village. They are dressed in garish costumes and wear funny yet intriguing masks on their faces. Live musicians play Kashmiri folk music. Haider, dressed as a joker wearing a mask, also dances along. Kids of the village enjoy the performance.

Arshia's car stops outside the village. She walks inside to find Haider dancing with full gusto with the group. She is happy to see him so cheerful. Haider notices her while dancing. He runs to her in joy.

He twirls her around as he keeps singing. She laughs seeing him in an upbeat mood. Suddenly, he sees the Salmans looking at them from behind a tree.

HAIDER

साले जासूस...

Bloody spies!

He grabs her hand and runs deeper into the village. Salman and Salman follow them. A chase begins - Haider manages to smartly evade the Salmans, who are now lost in the labyrinth of the village lanes. They run around but don't find them anywhere. A poem in a whispering voice starts to hum very softly on the soundtrack.

142 I/E. HOLLOW CHINAR TREE

A big chinar tree in the middle of the village square. In the claustrophobic confines of the hollow tree, Haider and Arshia stand in a tight embrace.

DISSOLVE TO:

143 INT. ROOM IN THE BHAAND VILLAGE - LATER

They kiss passionately and make love as the poem continues on the soundtrack.

144 INT. ROOM IN THE BHAAND VILLAGE - LATER

Post-coital scene. Under a quilt, Arshia rests her head on Haider's lap as he plays with her hair.

ARSHIA

सबको शक़ है कि तुम पागल हो रहे हो.

Everyone suspects you have gone insane.

Haider smiles.

HAIDER

शक़ पे है यकीन तो... यकीन पे है शक़ मुझे...

If what I suspect is to be believed, I suspect what I believe...

ARSHIA

मतलब?

What do you mean?

HAIDER

मतलब... रूहदार का अफ़साना सच्चा, या झूठी कहानी चाचा की... किसका झूठ झूठ है... किसके सच में सच नहीं...? है... कि है नहीं...? बस यही सवाल है. और सवाल का जवाब भी सवाल है.

I mean... Is there truth in Roohdaar's tale? Or is uncle's story all a lie? Whose lie is a lie? And whose truth lacks the truth? Does it exist or does it not? That is the question... The answer to that is also a question.

She looks at him confused.

ARSHIA

क्या?

What is it?

A streak of madness is seen in his eyes. He takes out the pistol from his bag and puts it on his heart and then on the temple.

HAIDER

दिल की अगर सुनूँ तो है, दिमाग की तो है नहीं... जान लूँ कि जान दूँ, मैं रहूँ... कि मैं नहीं?

If I listen to my heart... then yes... If I listen to my head... then no... Murder... or suicide? Should I live or should I not?

Arshia is shocked. She pulls the pistol from his hand.

ARSHIA
किसने दी ये तुम्हें?
Who gave this to you?

Haider tries to take it from her, she pulls it back.

ARSHIA
हैदर तुम ऐसा कुछ भी नहीं करोगे... उनकी बात सच निकले या झूठ...
Promise me... Haider... You will do no such thing.
Whether it's the truth or a lie... Promise me.

HAIDER
वापस दो.
Give it back...

ARSHIA
पहले क़सम खाओ मेरी.
Promise me.

Haider looks away. She puts his hand over her head.

ARSHIA
I have 'lovve-d' you more than my life.

Haider laughs.

HAIDER
LOWEDD नहीं LOVED.

He embraces her tightly and kisses.

HAIDER
बोलो LOVED... V और D softly.
Not 'lovve-d', it's 'loved'...

ARSHIA
LOWEDD.
Lovve-d.

Haider laughs again.

HAIDER
अच्छा बोलो.... Kicked.
Say.. Kicked.

ARSHIA
Kicckked.
Kick-ked.

HAIDER
बोलो plucked.
Now 'plucked'.

ARSHIA
Pluckkedd.
Pluck-ked.

HAIDER
Fucked.
Fucked.

ARSHIA
Fa...
Fu... 'Baster-ed'.

Arshia stops and hits him lovingly. They remain silent in a hug for a while.

ARSHIA

परसों निकाह है...

The weding is day after...

HAIDER

हम...

Hmm...

ARSHIA

तुम आओगे ना?

You're coming, right?

HAIDER

सौ फीसदी.... अपनी माँ का निकाह देखने का मौका किसी किसी को नसीब होता है.

100 per cent... Not everyone has the good fortune
of attending their own mother's wedding.

Arshia tries to smile. He takes the pistol back from her.

CUT TO:

145 I/E. KHURRAM'S HOME - DAY

A festive mood at home. The maulvi sits with some elderly people while Khurram is looking after the arrangements. Haider arrives. Khurram looks at him, a beat. He opens his arms, Haider walks up to him and hugs him tight.

CUT TO:

146 INT. KHURRAM'S HOUSE BEDROOM.

Haider reaches Ghazala's room. She looks beautiful in a bride's attire. Ghazala looks at him in the mirror. She turns and hugs him tight.

GHAZALA

जाना...

My angel...

They stand in silence.

GHAZALA

याद है... बचपन में तू क्या कहता था?
बड़ा होकर मौजे से निकाह करूँगा.

Remember, what you would say
when you were a child? 'When I grow up I will
marry my Mommy.'

She pulls herself back to look at him and laughs. Haider smiles too. She turns around and sits in front of the mirror to touch up.

GHAZALA

रोज़ रात को डॉक साहब और मेरे बीच आ के सो जाता था.

You would snuggle between
your father and me.

She looks at him in the mirror.

GHAZALA

वो मुझे छूते भी थे... तो लड़ता था उनसे...

Even if he touched me, you would fight with him.

HAIDER

अब तो उनका भाई आपको छूता है...
अब क्या करूँ?

Ah! Now his brother touches you...What does one say now?

Ghazala's smile fades out. Haider suddenly laughs.

HAIDER

आपको बाँटने को दिल नहीं करता मौजे...

Who would want to share you with the world?

He takes a bit of kohl on his index finger and puts it on her cheek.

HAIDER

ज़हर खूबसूरत हैं आप.

You are drop-dead gorgeous.

Ghazala smiles.

CUT TO:

147 INT. KHURRAM'S HOUSE LIVING ROOM - LATER

Khurram looks at Ghazala who is sitting with a few women across the room from him. The maulvi sings a verse from the Quran.

148 INT. KHURRAM'S HOUSE-LIVING ROOM-LATER

The ceremony continues in the other room. Arshia sits on a couch, she gathers her courage to speak to Parvez. A grim Parvez looks on.

ARSHIA

उन लोगों ने उसे एक पिस्तौल भी दी है... चाचा को मारने के लिए.
They have given him a pistol... to kill uncle Khurram...

Parvez is shocked.

CUT TO:

148A INT. BATHROOM OF GHAZALA'S BEDROOM

Haider hides his pistol inside the flush tank.

148B INT. KHURRAM'S HOUSE LIVING ROOM

The maulvi now faces Khurram.

MAULVI

खुर्रम मीर वलदीह हुसैन मीर आपको गज़ाला अख़्तर वालिद अख़बार खान से निकाह क़बूल है.

Khurram Hussain Meer... do you accept Ghazala Akhtar as your lawfully married wife?

KHURRAM

क़बूल है.

I do.

148C INT. GHAZALA'S BEDROOM

Parvez searches for the pistol everywhere in the room - inside the cupboard, Haider's rucksack, etc.

149 INT. KHURRAM'S HOME - LIVING ROOM

The maulvi turns to Ghazala.

MAULVI

गज़ाला अख़्तर दोख़्तरिह अकबर खान, आपको खुर्रम मीर वलदीह हुसैन मीर के साथ, बा मेहर 3 लाख रूपए, निकाह क़बूल है?

Ghazala Akhtar... Do you accept Khurram Hussain Meer as your lawfully married husband?

Ghazala keeps looking down. Haider looks at her while standing at the door. On his face we hear Ghazala's voice.

GHAZALA

क़बूल है.

I do.

A small cheer from the crowd. A looney smiles appears on Haider's face. Parvez enters and looks at Haider. The music from the next scene fades in.

CUT TO:

150 INT. AISHMUQAM SHRINE - EVENING

A festive mood. Tents are pitched, a small number of friends and dignitaries have gathered. The seating surrounds the central open space, like an amphitheatre.

Guests congratulate Ghazala and Khurram who sit at the centre, on two throne-like chairs. Parvez, with Arshia to his side, accompanies Khurram.

The Bhaand Pather begins. Masked entertainers come twirling in with the sounds of live instruments. The lead narrator, a masked Haider, begins the play. The players - the old king, the new king and the queen, along with their subjects.

The lyrics tell the story of the newly-crowned king after he betrayed and murdered his own brother, the older king.

The song tells of how the new king longed for the queen and would do anything to have her. The old king was considered a traitor by the feudal lord who conquered their kingdom. His brother was hand-in-glove with the feudal lord, therefore they both conspired to trap the old king and killed him to ensure that the kingdom and the queen would be the new king's forever.

There are details of the killing, with the body being thrown from the 'Zero Bridge'.

Ghazala and Khurram are visibly disturbed. Khurram, seething from inside, doesn't flinch an inch. With a final dance move Haider kneels before Khurram to end the powerful performance. The audience is silent. A beat.

Khurram claps gently. He inches closer towards Haider and whispers, glaring into his eyes.

KHURRAM

कहानी बहुत खूब है तुम्हारे पाथेर की...

Such a brilliant story!

Haider is silent. Khurram pulls down his mask, to reveal his teary-eyed face. Khurram wipes off his tears.

KHURRAM

किसने लिखी? ज़हूर हुसैन ने या रूहदार ने? हम?

Who wrote this play? Zahoor Hussain? Or was it Roohdaar?

Haider's eyes are locked with him. Khurram smiles and looks around and whispers.

KHURRAM

पिस्टल भी तो दी उन्होंने तुम्हें एक मुझे मारने के लिए. चायनीज .22. कहाँ छुपा रखी है?

And how do you like their gift of a pistol... to kill me?

Haider is shocked, his eyes dart towards Arshia who is equally stunned. She looks at Parvez who avoids her gaze. Khurram turns his face around.

KHURRAM

तुम्हारे दिमाग का चारा बस अब एक जगह हो सकता है...
पागलखाने में...

Shall we have him treated? In a psychiatric hospital?

Haider is seething with anger. Khurram looks at Parvez and nods. Parvez nods to a policeman in turn. Ghazala looks at Khurram.

GHAZALA

खुर्रम... क्या हो रहा है ये.

What's going on here?

Haider looks at the policeman walking towards him. He suddenly runs. The policeman chases him.

GHAZALA

(screams)

हैदर...

Haider...

He is gone. Haider dodges everyone, hits a few of them while escaping through the alleys. He takes a turn and suddenly Salman and Salman appear from nowhere. One of them hits him hard on the back of his head with a wooden log. Haider bangs into a wall and passes out.

CUT TO:

151 INT. KHURRAM'S HOME - SPARE BEDROOM - EVENING

Haider lies on the bed unconscious. A doctor administers an injection on his arm. Ghazala sits next to him, silently crying and brushing his hair gently.

Khurram and Parvez stand closer.

DOCTOR

It's Post-Traumatic Stress Disorder… PTSD. He needs psychiatric care. मैने हॉस्पिटल में बात कर ली है. कल सुवह कर्फ्यू खुलते ही इसे हस्पताल में एडमिट कर देंगे.

It's Post Traumatic Stress Disorder... PTSD. He needs psychiatric care. I've spoken to the doctors at the psychiatric hospital… We'll move him there the moment the curfew is lifted in the morning.

PARVEZ

ये अगर जाग गया तो भाग जाएगा.

If he wakes up, he'll make a run for it.

The doctor wraps up his instruments.

DOCTOR

Heavy dose दिया है मैने. नहीं जागेगा.

I have sedated him well. He won't wake up for hours.

Parvez and Khurram look at each other.

CUT TO:

152 INT-EXT. KHURRAM'S HOME

Parvez and the doctor drive away in his jeep.

INSIDE

Khurram sits next to Ghazala who still brushes Haider's hair.

GHAZALA
जो इसे लग रहा है वो सच है क्या?
Is what he suspects true?

Khurram is quiet. He turns her around, holds her face.

KHURRAM
आपको क्या लगता है...?
What do you think?

A beat. She hugs him and rests her head on his chest.

GHAZALA
झूठ... तुम क़त्ल नहीं कर सकते... वो भी अपने भाई का... कभी नहीं.
Utter lies... You cannot kill anybody... let alone your own brother...

A touch of guilt overcomes Khurram's face as he holds Ghazala. He looks at Haider sleeping like a baby.

CUT TO:

153 INT. PARVEZ HOME - NIGHT

Arshia lies on the bed of her room, looking nowhere. Her eyes are red after hours of crying. The plateful of food remains untouched on the table. The jeep stopping outside in the porch breaks her trance.

Parvez knocks gently on the door of her room.

PARVEZ
अर्शी...
Arshee...

There is no response. He knocks again.

PARVEZ
अर्शी... दरवाज़ा खोलो...
Arshee... Open the door...

No response again.

PARVEZ
अर्शी बेटा... तुम्हे ग़लतफ़हमी हुई है.
You misunderstand me.

Arshia suddenly screams from inside.

ARSHIA
नहीं... आपने धोखा दिया है मुझे... इस्तेमाल किया है मुझे... You use-d me.. आपको हैदर की सलामती से कोई मतलब नहीं है... आप उसके जरिए उन लोगों तक पहुँचना चाहते है जिन्होंने खुर्रम को एक्सपोज किया है. इस सब में हैदर अगर मर भी गया तो आपको कोई फर्क़ नहीं पड़ेगा.

No! You betrayed me. You took advantage of my trust... You used me... You don't care for Haider's life... You want to use him to catch those people... who unmasked the truth about Khurram... You don't care if Haider has to die.

She sobs as it hits Parvez hard. He closes his eyes and takes a deep breath.

PARVEZ

दरवाज़ा खोलो और बात करो मुझसे... मेरा नज़रिया देखने की भी तो कोशिश करो...

Open the door and let me explain...Try to see my point.

Arshia cries more.

ARSHIA

ना मुझे आपका नज़रिया देखना है और ना ही आपकी सूरत. कभी नहीं.

I don't want to get your point... I don't want to see you... ever!

She falls on the bed as Parvez stands at the door, helpless.

CUT TO:

154 INT. KHURRAM'S HOUSE - NIGHT

Haider sleeps on the bed. Ghazala sleeps next to him on a chair, her hand over his chest.

The door opens, Hilaal stands there in prison clothes, his hands and legs chained. He slowly walks to the bed and sits next to Haider and slowly takes Ghazala's hand off his chest and whispers.

HILAAL

हैदर... मेरा इंतक़ाम लेना... मेरे भाई से...

Haider...Avenge my betrayal and my most foul and unnatural murder by my serpent of a brother...

Ghazala slowly wakes up. Hilaal looks at her expressionless. She is shocked. Hilaal looks back at the sleeping Haider and brushes his hair gently.

HILAAL

उसकी उन दो आँखों में गोलियाँ दागना, जिन आँखों से उसने तेरी माँ पर फरेब डाले थे....

Aim your bullets at his treacherous eyes... Those deceitful eyes which entrapped your mother.

Haider's eyes snap open. He finds himself alone in the empty room, his body full of sweat. Ghazala sleeps next to him on a chair, her hand over his chest. He slowly puts her hand away, looks at the time - 5:02 AM. It's still dark outside, at a distance we hear the faint sounds of the morning 'azaan'. He gets up and walks to the bathroom. He lifts the upper part of the flush tank and takes out the Chinese pistol. He comes out and looks at Ghazala, she is still asleep.

CUT TO:

155 INT. KHURRAM'S HOME - CORRIDOR - DAWN

Haider tiptoes quietly across the dark corridor, he makes his way to the master bedroom when he notices light from the prayer room seeping through the open door.

156 INT. KHURRAM'S HOME - PRAYER ROOM

He peeps into the room to see Khurram kneeling down in prayer, his back towards Haider. Khurram murmurs the prayer, his eyes open, but focused on a single point right in front of him. He is almost in a trance.

KHURRAM

अै मेरे परवरदिगार तेरा मुजरिम हूँ... बहुत शर्मसार हूँ... अपने जिस्म से खून की बू आती है मुझे मौत की बू...

My lord, my crime, my sin stinks the skies, the earth... I fail even to bow in prayer despite my punishing guilt... My brother's blood covers my cursed hand...

Haider creeps in towards Khurram, pistol in hand.

CUT TO:

157 EXT. KHURRAM'S HOME - CORRIDOR

Parvez drives up at the house, followed by Salman and Salman in a jeep. The guards salute Parvez, as he steps out of his Ambassador.

CUT TO:

158 INT. KHURRAM'S HOME - PRAYER ROOM

Khurram still deep in his prayer-trance.

KHURRAM

अहंकारी की इस... ज़िल्लत से नजात दिला दे, मेरे मौला... बदले में जो चाहे ले ले... मेरी इज़्ज़त दौलत शोहरत... सब कुछ ले ले... मेरी बदरक रूह धो के... मुझे फिर से पाक कर दे मेरे मौला ...

All the wealth, all the power, all the fame.... Wash me clean as snow with the rain of your mercy, My Lord! Your mercy is greater than my rank crime, My Lord!

Haider is now right behind him, his hand trembles as he raises the pistol to aim. Tears start to form in Khurram's eyes.

CUT TO:

159 INT. KHURRAM'S HOME

The old domestic help who is outside collecting the day's newspaper and milk, greets Parvez and lets them into the house.

The Salmans and Parvez look towards the room.

CUT TO:

160 INT. KHURRAM'S HOME - PRAYER ROOM

Haider has the pistol aimed right at the back of Khurram's head. Tears roll off Khurram's face now. His eyes full of regret and sorrow, still focused at a single spot, they don't flinch an inch. Haider's finger is on the trigger.

KHURRAM

मैं गुनाहगार हूँ. तेरी रहमत की सरहद नहीं. मुझे बक़्श दे, मेरे खुदा!

Dear God! You alone can forgive my horrible murder...

Haider can't pull the trigger.

CUT TO:

161 INT. KHURRAM'S HOUSE LIVING ROOM

Haider comes out of the prayer room to face Salman and Salman along with Parvez standing at the door.

Parvez lunges at him, Haider's pistol flies away. Salman and Salman run to overpower Haider.

Inside - Khurram ends his prayers.

Outside - chaos of voices as the Salmans along with Parvez struggle to overpower Haider.

Ghazala comes out hearing the commotion. Khurram walks out still wearing his prayer cap. Salman and Salman hold a fuming Haider. Parvez ties Haider's hands with his red muffler. The other guards from outside come running in.

GHAZALA

क्या हुआ... (to the Salmans) छोड़ उसे.

What are you doing? Let go of him...

Parvez shows the pistol to Khurram.

PARVEZ

हम वक़्त पे आ गए... वर्ना...

We caught him in time... or he might have...

Khurram looks at Haider, who smiles.

HAIDER

तू नमाज़ में था इस लिए नहीं मारा... मार देता तो तुझ जैसे सुअर को भी जन्नत मिल जाती.

I didn't kill you because you were in prayer...
Even a ghastly sinner would enter
heaven if killed in prayer.

Khurram wipes his damp eyes and looks back at Ghazala. She walks to Haider, shocked.

HAIDER

तुझे मारूँगा... जब तू गुनाह में होगा, दुआ में नहीं...

I will kill you when you are in sin... not when you are in prayer...

GHAZALA

हैदर... तू सच में पागल हो गया है!

Haider... you have really gone insane!

Khurram nods, Salman and Salman drag him out as he screams.

HAIDER

तेरी दोनों आँखों में गोलियाँ दागूँगा खुर्रम, जिन आँखों से तूने मेरी मौजे पर फरेब डाली है.

I aim my bullets at your treacherous eyes, Khurram... those deceitful eyes that entrapped my mother.

Ghazala cries as Khurram hugs her.

CUT TO:

162 EXT. KHURRAM'S HOME - LATER

Salman and Salman escort Haider to the jeep, his hands tied with Parvez's red muffler. Two armed guards sit behind with Haider as Salman 1 locks the back. Salman 2 starts the jeep. Parvez comes to the window and hands Salman 1, Haider's rucksack.

PARVEZ

दूर से मारना, और पीठ पे मारना....

Shoot from a distance... And shoot him in the back.

Salman nods, the jeep drives away as Ghazala cries at the window resting her head on Khurram's shoulder.

CUT TO:

163 EXT. ISOLATED ROAD - LATER

The jeep travels on a bumpy barren terrain. Salman and Salman sing along to a hit Salman Khan song blaring on the music system. Behind, the guards sit casually with weapons on their laps while Haider is seated on the opposite side.

The road gets bumpier, Salman tries to control the vehicle. Haider seizes the moment and pounces onto the guards. A fist-fight between them. The car swerves out of control, one guard falls over losing his grip on his gun, Haider grabs it, pulls the trigger and shoots randomly. The bullets hit both of them and blood splashes on the glass screen separating the back from the front. Salman completely loses control of the jeep, crashing into a tree head-on.

Haider bangs into the wall of the jeep and gets knocked out due to the collision. Salman and Salman take a peek behind to see Haider lie unconscious, they quickly get out and head back to unlock the door. Salman 1 unlocks the door as Salman 2 holds the pistol. Haider violently kicks it open pushing Salman 1 back. He bangs into Salman 2, his pistol flies away.

Haider climbs out of the jeep pointing the AK 47 towards Salman and Salman.

SALMAN 1

हैदर यार देख... हम तेरे दोस्त हैं यार... तू जो बोलेगा हम करेंगे.

Haider don't! We'll do as you say...

HAIDER

हाथ खोल...

Free my hands.

One of the Salmans come forward and opens the knot of the

muffler. He suddenly butts his head on his nose. Haider falls back, they pick the gun and shoot at him but the magazine is over. A beat.

HAIDER
चुटज़पा!
Chutzpah!

Haider lunges for the pistol lying nearby. Both the Salmans run for their life.

Haider aims and fires, missing both of them, he fires a couple more times, missing again. They cackle like a couple of hyenas, calling him names. Haider puts the gun back into his back pocket and picks a big stone.

The Salmans keep running. Suddenly we hear a THUD!

Salman 1 falls to the ground immediately, blood oozes out from the back of his head. Salman 2 turns to him. Another

THUD! He screams in pain as a stone hits him hard on the face. His nose now bleeding, he looks up at the distance to see Haider running towards him with a few rocks in his hands. Salman 2 runs. Salman 1 tries to get up but another stone hits him hard. He falls again. Haider aims another rock at Salman 1, it knocks him down as well. With every throw Haider is more violent and fierce.

Teary-eyed Salman 2 drags himself over to Salman 1's body.

SALMAN

सलमान!... सलमान...!

Salman! Salman!

He shakes Salman's lifeless body violently, his own face full of blood. Haider catches up behind them. Salman cries for mercy. Haider picks up a large stone with both hands, raises it in the air and swings downwards.

CUT TO:

164 I/E. PCO AT A SMALL VILLAGE NEAR HIGHWAY - DAY

Haider, hiding his face behind Parvez's muffler, speaks into the phone.

HAIDER

खुर्रम बच गया... लेकिन मैने तीन पुलिस वालों को मार दिया.

Khurram is still alive. But I've killed three cops.

165 INT. HIDEOUT

Roohdaar and Zahoor listen to him on the speaker of the phone.

ROOHDAAR

माशाअल्लाह...

I heard...

A young studious-looking boy with thick glasses on his nose carefully assembles an explosive suicide vest - placing ball bearings, nails, screws, etc., on a thick fabric and covering it with another one.

ROOHDAAR

अभी कहाँ है तू?

Where are you now?

HAIDER

पाम्पोर हाईवे.

Pampore highway.

Roohdaar looks at Zahoor, who nods.

ROOHDAAR

तुझे सरहद पार जाना होगा. ट्रेनिंग के लिए.

You will need to cross the border for training...

Haider listens to him quietly.

ROOHDAAR

जिस क़ब्रिस्तान पे मिले थे हमसे, वहीं पहुँच, हम रबता करेंगे.

Get to the graveyard where
we met first. We'll get in touch...

HAIDER

जी.

Okay.

ROOHDAAR

सलाम आलेकुम.

Peace be upon you.

HAIDER

वालेकुम सलाम.

Peace be upon you.

Haider puts the receiver back and moves to go out but stops. He looks back at the phone.

CUT TO:

166 EXT. KHURRAM'S HOME - DAY

The telephone rings loudly. Ghazala picks up the receiver.

GHAZALA

हेलो.

Hello.

There is silence at the other end, only the sound of breathing.

GHAZALA

हेलो हैदर... कहाँ है तू? हस्पताल पहुँच गया? हैदर?

Hello Haider... Where are you? Have you reached the hospital? Haider...

We hear Haider's choking voice at the other end.

HAIDER

अलग होने के और भी तो रास्ते थे मौजे... खून क्यों करा डाला आपने मेरे ओबुजी का?

There are other ways to part... Why did you have to get my father killed?

His words fall on Ghazala like a rock. She breaks down.

GHAZALA

या खुदा...

God!

She howls and falls on the ground, speaks after a while.

GHAZALA

तेरी क़सम जाना... ये झूठ है.

This is not true! I swear upon God... this is not true!

She cries as Haider takes the speaker off his ear, closes his eyes to resist his emotions. He puts the phone back on his mouth and whispers.

HAIDER

मैं जा रहा हूँ मौजे...

I'm going mother.

GHAZALA

कहाँ?

Where?

Haider is quiet. Ghazala's voice is almost choked.

GHAZALA

हैदर सरहद पार जा रहा है तू?

You're crossing the border?

Haider remains quiet.

GHAZALA

तुझे कुछ हुआ तो मैं नहीं बचुँगी हैदर.

It is a fatal trek..
I won't bear losing you..

Haider is still quiet.

GHAZALA

एक बार मिल तो ले मुझसे... जाना... मैं रोकूँगी नहीं तुझे इस बार...
क़सम से... एक बार मिल ले बस... जाना...

At least, meet me once...
I won't stop you this time. I promise...Meet me once.

She cries as Haider listens silently.

CUT TO:

167 EXT. HILAAL'S HOME - DAY

An autorickshaw stops in front of the burnt house. Ghazala comes out wearing a pheran. Her head is covered with a scarf and eyes with big sunglasses. She looks at the house. Emotions run through her veins.

CUT TO:

168 INT. HILAAL'S HOME

Ghazala enters the house, her feet crushing the debris of the charred wood.

She looks at the mirror on the wall. Its cracked from the middle. Haider's voice comes from behind.

HAIDER

दो चेहरे हैं आपके मौजे.

My Janus-faced mother.

She turns to see Haider walking behind. He comes closer and turns her around to face the mirror. He holds her face from the chin and tightens the grip with each word he speaks.

HAIDER

ये बाँयें वाला मासूम है और वो दाँयें वाला चोर. इससे आपने फतिहा पढ़ा और इससे निकाह क़बूल किया.

Such innocence in one face; such deceit in the other..
This face reads the prayers at my father's funeral..
That one glows with repeating marital vows to
Khurram.

GHAZALA

तुझे बहकाया है उन लोगों ने. डॉक साहब की मौत से हमारा कोई वास्ता नहीं है.

I am not to blame for your father's death.

Haider laughs aloud.

HAIDER

झूठ का दूसरा नाम है... औरत... ओबुजी के क़ब्र के फूल सूखे भी नहीं थे कि आपने खुर्रम के साथ घर बसा लिया.

Oh! How sad to see a mother lie... The flowers on father's grave were still fresh... and you rushed into Khurram's marital bed.

Ghazala's face is distorted now because of the force of the grip of his hand.

HAIDER

सबको पता है... आप दोनों ने मिल के ओबुजी के क़त्ल की साज़िश की है.

The world knows you and Khurram conspired to murder my father.

Ghazala is shocked.

GHAZALA

ये झूठ है....

These are utter lies...

HAIDER

इख्लाख़ उस रात हमारे घर में छुपा था. ये बात आपके अलावा किसी और को पता नहीं थी. फौज का मुखबिर खुर्रम था... और खुर्रम की मुखबिर आप.

Ikhlaakh was hiding in our

house that fateful day... Khurram was an informant for the army... and you were his informer.

CUT TO:

Flashback:

169 INT. BATHROOM-NIGHT

Ghazala throws up violently in the wash basin. She stops after a while and looks at herself in the mirror. The telephone rings outside.

170 INT. STUDY

Ghazala looks at the ringing telephone. She looks around to find herself alone, she answers the call.

GHAZALA

हेलो...

Hello.

On the other line is Khurram.

KHURRAM

ग़ज़ाला... आज चाँद देखा तुमने?

You had to be home. The moon wouldn't dare shine in the skies.

Ghazala sobs quietly.

KHURRAM

ग़ज़ाला... क्या हुआ?

What happened?

GHAZALA

बहुत डर लग रहा है मुझे खुर्रम...

I'm scared, Khurram.

She breaks down uncontrollably.

KHURRAM

क्यों??

What happened?

GHAZALA

हिलाल... आज इख़्लाख़ लतीफ को घर ले आया है.

Hilaal's brought Ikhlaakh home today.

KHURRAM

इख़्लाख़ लतीफ!!

Ikhlaakh Latif!

Ghazala speaks to him but her voice-over from the next scene fades in on the soundtrack.

CUT TO:

Flashback ends:

171 INT. HILAAL'S HOME

They both sit on the burnt wooden staircase. Haider looks on, speechless.

GHAZALA

डॉक्टर साहब की मौत नहीं चाही थी मैने... कभी नहीं... उनके लिए मेरे दिल में ज़हर नहीं था...

I never wanted to harm or hurt your father. I did not hate him.

She looks away.

HAIDER

और खुर्रम के लिए? खुर्रम के लिए क्या था...?

And Khurram? What about him?

GHAZALA

हाँ... खुर्रम के लिए मोहब्बत... थी. हमेशा से...

But I have always loved Khurram.

Haider pulls her face to look at him.

CUT TO:

172 EXT. HILAAL'S HOME

Parvez's car passes through the lane adjacent to Hilaal's burnt house. He notices a red-coloured fabric lying at the corner of the road. He asks his driver to stop the car.

Parvez walks down to the corner and picks the cloth, it is his red muffler woven by Arshia, the same he tied Haider's hands with. He looks towards the burnt house.

CUT TO

173 INT. HILAAL'S HOME

Haider gets up to leave. Ghazala whispers from behind.

GHAZALA

अब क्या करेगा तू?

Now what will do?

HAIDER

वही जो आप करती थीं... इंतज़ार.

I'll wait eagerly...

He turns around and bends down to look into her eyes.

HAIDER

आपके दुबारा बेवा होने का.

For you to be a widow again.

CUT TO:

174 INT. HILAAL'S HOME

Parvez tiptoes inside the house. Holding his revolver, ready to shoot.

175 INT. HILAAL'S HOME

Ghazala is crestfallen.

GHAZALA

एक एहसान करेगा मुझ पर?

Do me a favour?

Haider looks at her with questioning eyes.

GHAZALA

बहुत मनहूस पेशानी है मेरी...

I am tired of my wretched life...

She clasps his hands which hold the pistol and puts it on her forehead.

GHAZALA

दाग़ दे.

Kill me...

HAIDER

आपकी ज़िदगी ही आपकी सज़ा है मौजे.

Your life is your punishment.

Parvez peeps through the slit of the door to find Haider holding the pistol at Ghazala's forehead. He stumbles behind the door. Haider turns and shoots at the door. The bullet hits him right in the forehead through the door. He falls on his security guard standing behind him. They both come crashing down on the ground. Ghazala screams. Haider runs through the other exit as Parvez's security guard shoots at him.

CUT TO:

176 EXT. SRINAGAR AIRPORT- DAY

An Indian Airlines aircraft lands on the runway and soon comes to a halt. The ground crew attaches the mobile staircase. The hatch swings open, one by one passengers begin to exit the plane, Liyaqat one of them.

CUT TO:

177 INT. PARVEZ'S HOME - LATER

Arshia sits next to Parvez's dead body. Her eyes are blank as she fans the flies away from the dead body. A few friends and family members have gathered to mourn the death. Ghazala stands at a corner, Khurram comes from behind.

KHURRAM

इस मौत की ज़िम्मेदार आप भी हैं... सब कुछ जानते बूझते आप मिलने गईं हैदर से... मुझसे छुप कर... आप का बेटा उस तरफ चला गया है गज़ाला... वहशी भेड़िया बन चुका है वो...

You are also responsible for this death... Despite knowing everything, you went to meet Haider... behind my back... Haider has gone to the other side, Ghazala... he is a blood-thirsty wolf now...

Ghazala looks into his eyes straight.

GHAZALA

शुक्र है आस्तीन का साँप नहीं बना...

At least he does not bite the hand that feeds him...

A beat.

KHURRAM

मेरी मुहब्बत झूठी नहीं है गज़ाला.

My love is not a lie, Ghazala.

Ghazala smiles sadly.

GHAZALA

मुहब्बत जान देती है जान लेती नहीं...

You give up life in love, not take it away...

A beat.

KHURRAM

आपको मुझसे से ज़्यादा अपने बेटे पर यक़ीन है... वो पागल है पागल.

Your son has crossed over to the other side...
He's lost it.

Ghazala nods.

GHAZALA

जी. पर दगाबाज़ नहीं है.

Yes... but thankfully he's not a traitor...

They look at each other in silence.

We hear a car door slam shut. Moments later Liyaqat storms into the room. His handbag slung on his shoulder. He freezes at the doorstep. Arshia looks at him, suddenly she gets up and runs to him. She cries in his arms as tears roll off his cheeks.

Liyaqat walks to Parvez's body, kneels down, holds his lifeless hand and breaks down.

Khurram comes up from behind and rests his hand on Liyaqat's shoulder to console him. He looks up behind. A beat.

Liyaqat stands and pushes Khurram back violently.

LIYAQAT

हैदर कहाँ है?

Where is Haider?

Khurram tries to pacify him.

KHURRAM

लकी... सब्र करो.

Liyaqat... calm down.

Liyaqat pins him against the wall and holds him by the throat.

LIYAQAT

कहाँ है?

Where is he?

People move to intervene but Liyaqat is too aggressive to control. Suddenly Khurram punches him hard in the belly. Liyaqat rolls over in pain.

KHURRAM

जहाँ भी होगा बचेगा नहीं.

Wherever he is... he will not survive.

He walks to Liyaqat and hugs him. His eyes meet Ghazala's.

KHURRAM

उनके चहरूम से पहले हैदर की मैयत उठाऊँगा मैं.

I will not rest, till I see him inside a coffin.

Ghazala's face goes pale. Liyaqat cries on his shoulder like a baby.

CUT TO:

178 EXT. PARVEZ'S HOME - LATER

Funeral starts from Parvez's house. The coffin is lifted by four people, Liyaqat and Khurram among them. The priest chants verses from Quran as it heads for the graveyard.

A soft humming of a female voice-overlaps the soundtrack.

CUT TO:

179 INT. PARVEZ HOME PORCH - LATER

Only a few ladies of the neighbourhood are present in the

house. A devastated Arshia sitting alone on the porch, hums a Kashmiri song of Habba Khatoon. She pulls out strands of wool from the muffler she had woven for her father. Her belongings from the bag - a diary a photo album etc. - are lying on the floor next to her. Ghazala comes from behind and sits beside her.

GHAZALA

दोनों के हाथ में पिस्तौल थी... हैदर ने गोली ना चलायी होती तो परवेज़ भाई ने उसे मार दिया होता.

Both of them had guns in their hands...
Haider fired first.

Arshia keeps humming, oblivious to Ghazala's presence. Ghazala sees a photograph of Haider and Arshia kept in between the pages of the diary. She picks up the notebook and looks at the photograph. Her voice chokes as she speaks.

GHAZALA

सब उसके खून के प्यासे हैं... अब उसका बचना... बहुत मुशकिल है.

Everyone wants to kill him. I know he
won't make it.

As she keeps the notebook back a piece of paper falls on the ground. The same chit Roohdaar had passed off to Arshia.

Ghazala looks at the name written over it - 'Roohdaar' - and a phone number scribbled against it. She looks back at Arshia. She continues to sing while pulling out the strands of the wool.

CUT TO:

180 INT. HIDEOUT - DAY

Roohdaar shows the suicide vest to Zahoor on a hanger.

Zahoor looks inside the vest - it is full of explosives. The young studious boy who was working on it hands over a switch button attached to it. Roohdaar looks at it and presses the button.

ROOHDAAR

बूम...

Boom...

All of them laugh. A young man comes to Roohdaar with the phone.

YOUNG MAN

डॉक साहब की बीवी का फोन है.

It's the doctor's wife on the line.

Zahoor looks on surprised. Roohdaar smiles.

CUT TO

Pre-lap sound: We hear the sounds of shovels digging through dry soil. They create a perfect rhythmic pattern with each other. A dry soulful voice sings in sync with the sounds.

FADE IN:

181 EXT. ISLAMIC GRAVEYARD - DAY

The old man sings standing inside a grave, throwing soil out with every swing of his shovel. He is the gravedigger. Behind him in three adjacent graves are two other old men, Mohsin and Ali, and a young boy, Akram, twelve.

All three old men dig and sing in sync. A song of life and death, of slaughter and massacre, of burial and exhumation.

A mysterious figure walks up to them. The gravedigger looks up. It's Haider.

GRAVEDIGGER

हैदर... तुम्हारा ही इंतज़ार हो रहा है सवेरे से...

Haider... Where have you been? Everyone has been waiting for you since morning.

He looks at the kids. They smile at him.

GRAVEDIGGER

आओ... अपनी कबर खोदो... और सो जाओ...

Come dig your grave and lie down...

Haider smiles.

Later.

Haider digs along with the gravediggers. His shovel hits something hard inside the ground. He digs it out. It's a skull of a human being. Everyone stops and looks at it.

AKRAM

दादू, सारी खोपड़ियाँ हँसती क्यों रहती हैं.

Grandpa... why do all the skulls have smiling faces?

GRAVEDIGGER

पता नहीं पर तेरी रोती हुई मिलेगी. चल खोद चुपचाप.

Yours will surely be a crying one. Shut up and dig.

Haider goes close to Akram.

HAIDER

क्योंकि मर के ही समझ में आता है कि ज़िंदा थे तो जिए नहीं और मर के भी बचे नहीं. आया समझ?

Because only after one is dead, one realizes one never really lived. And even after death there is no escape... Got it?

He nods in the negative. Ali brings the water in an earthen pot.

HAIDER

जिस्म गल के मिट्टी बन जाता है. और मिट्टी से बनते हैं खिलौने, घड़े, सुराही. चाहे सिकन्दर हो या अकबर, हिटलर हो या गाँधी... आख़िर में मिट्टी ही बनता है.

The body turns into soil... The soil is made into vessels, pots and toys... Whether it's Alexander or Akbar... Hitler or Gandhi... We all turn into dirt.

He pours water for the old gravedigger who drinks by making a cup in his palm.

HAIDER

हो सकता है जिस सुराही से तुम्हारे दादाजी पानी पी रहे हैं, वो सिकन्दर के जिस्म की मिट्टी से बनी हो.

Who knows... this vessel your grandpa is drinking tea from... could be made of Alexander's body...

All of them laugh together.

HAIDER

भले ही दुनिया जीती हो कभी. आज तो क़ब्रिस्तान में पानी पिलाता घूम रहा है...

He may have conquered the world... but today he is at the graveyard serving tea for us...

They laugh more.

CUT TO:

182 INT. ISLAMIC GRAVEYARD - NIGHT

The gravedigger cooks something on an earthen stove. He looks at Haider and smiles.

GRAVEDIGGER

तेरी आँखें बिल्कुल मेरे बड़े बेटे की तरह हैं.

Your eyes are just like my eldest son's...

Haider looks at him and smiles sadly.

GRAVEDIGGER

रोई रोई, उदास सी... कशमीर की तरह...

Teary-eyed, sad... just like kashmir...

HAIDER

कहाँ है वो?

Where is he?

GRAVEDIGGER

बाहर... चिनार के नीचे दफ़न है.

Outside, buried below the chinar tree...

Haider's face hardens. The gravedigger goes back to cooking.

GRAVEDIGGER

आर्मी ज़िंदा ले गई थी घर से, पुलिस मुर्दा लाई वापस. खुदकुशी कर ली उसने जेल में...

The army picked him up alive... and the police brought him back... dead... he committed suicide in jail...

Haider is speechless.

CUT TO:

183 INT. PARVEZ'S HOME - LATER

Arshia lies on Parvez's bed, holding his pistol in her hands under her cheeks - like a pillow. Nothing remains of the pullover but loose strings, which lie spread all over her. She still hums the song.

CUT TO:

184 INT. ISLAMIC GRAVEYARD - DIGGER'S HOME - MORNING

Haider wakes up to the sounds of chants. At the window he sees that a small funeral procession has entered the graveyard. He recognizes one of Parvez's servants amongst the handful of people. One of the gravediggers walks in, Haider still looking out of the window.

HAIDER

किसका जनाज़ा है...?

Whose funeral is it?

AKRAM

वो जो है ना... वो लड़का...

That man over there...

He points out to Liyaqat at a distance. Haider is surprised to see him visibly distraught.

AKRAM

उसकी बहन है... खुदकुशी कर ली उसने... कल.

His sister... she commited suicide last night...

Haider is devastated.

185 EXT. ISLAMIC GRAVEYARD

The maulvi begins the ritual. Haider comes in trudging from behind Liyaqat, completely defeated and crying.

HAIDER

अर्शी...

Arshee...

He kneels down before her. Liyaqat can't believe his eyes. He trembles with anger as Haider holds her dead body, which is covered with a white shroud. Liyaqat turns to the servant and whispers.

LIYAQAT

(to servant)

खुर्रम साब को इत्तला करो... जल्दी.

Inform Khurram... Quickly!

The servant makes a run for it. Liyaqat comes forth and violently kicks Haider. He falls away on the ground.

Liyaqat kicks Haider repeatedly as he tries to reach Arshia. Finally Haider retaliates and pushes him hard, Liyaqat topples over near the grave.

Haider walks back and holds Arshia's dead body covered in the shroud. Liyaqat, raging with fury, runs back and starts hitting Haider who is not ready to leave Arshia's body.

The maulvi and others scatter in fear as the fight gets brutal. Upon seeing this, Mohsin runs to the entrance of the graveyard compound to look for the gravedigger. Liyaqat picks up a shovel and hits Haider hard on the back of his head. He falls down as Arshia's body falls into the dug-up grave.

186 EXT. ISLAMIC GRAVEYARD - ENTRANCE

Outside the compound, the gravedigger is with Akram, helping him climb into his school bus. From behind he hears Mohsin's voice calling out to him.

The gravedigger turns to see him as Akram's bus drives away.

CUT' TO:

187 EXT. ISLAMIC GRAVEYARD

A bloodied Haider crawls on the ground towards the grave.

Liyaqat towers above as he showers more kicks and blows. Liyaqat raises the shovel for a final blow.

A tombstone lies near the dug-up grave, Haider grabs it and with one mighty swing hits Liyaqat straight across the head, immediately knocking him out cold. Liyaqat drops dead on the ground.

A weak and bloodied Haider gets up and walks towards the grave. He embraces Arshia's lifeless body.

CUT TO:

188 EXT. ISLAMIC GRAVEYARD

The gravedigger and the other two old men run towards the graveyard. Haider still holds Arshia in his arms and cries.

CUT TO:

189 EXT. ISLAMIC GRAVEYARD - DIGGER'S HOME

Ali unbolts a wooden plank and pulls out thick covers to reveal a large arsenal of weapons.

In another room, the gravedigger listens to Zahoor on his telephone. Behind, Haider sits with Arshia's body in his arms.

ZAHOOR

(off-screen)

कुछ भी हो जाए, वो लड़का ज़िंदा रहना चाहिए... जितनी जल्दी हो सके वहाँ से निकालो.

Come what may... the boy should live... Get out of there as soon as you can.

Down below, Mohsin and Ali are loading their old Fiat car with weapons.

GRAVEDIGGER

इफ़रात असलाह है ज़हूर. गाड़ी में आड़ा भी नहीं आएगा.

We have too many weapons, Zahoor... they won't fit in the car.

ZAHOOR

(off-screen)

जितना भी आए लेकर निकलो... अभी...

Take whatever will fit in the car and leave... Now!

The gravedigger hears the rumbling of some vehicles outside. He looks out the window to see several armoured vehicles approaching the compound.

GRAVEDIGGER

ज़हूर... अब हम नहीं निकल सकते यहाँ से...

Zahoor, it is too late.

CUT TO:

190 EXT. ISLAMIC GRAVEYARD

Khurram drives into the compound with Ikhwaan soldiers in various armoured vehicles. They notice Liyaqat's dead body at one of the graves. Khurram signals to two soldiers to retrieve the body.

Those two run towards the body, when suddenly two quick rounds of gunfire hit them and knock them down.

Alarmed, Khurram and gang take cover behind a rock. They look towards the structure.

191 INT. ISLAMIC GRAVEYARD - DIGGER'S HOME

The nozzle of an AK 47 stealthily peeps out from the second-floor window. Ali is behind the gun aiming at the two dead bodies.

192 EXT. ISLAMIC GRAVEYARD

Ikhwaan soldiers stealthily tiptoe towards the back of the house

The gravedigger peeps out the window and fires from his AK47. The Ikhwaanis retreat.

193 EXT. ISLAMIC GRAVEYARD

The Ikhwaans get closer by hiding behind trees and graves in front of the house. At every chance they get they open fire, only to be met with retaliatory fire from the windows.

194 INT. ISLAMIC GRAVEYARD - DIGGER'S HOME

Mohsin has taken position at a window and is unleashing an onslaught of gun-fire towards the Ikhwaan soldiers.

All the while Haider holds Arshia's body and softly reads a poem to her.

195 I/E. ISLAMIC GRAVEYARD

By now a full-fledged battle is taking place between the Ikhwaans and the gravedigger family.

Two Ikhwaani soldiers manage to reach and hide below the place where Ali was firing from. As Ali opens the window, the two Ikhwaan soldiers shower bullets. Ali screams and falls back. The gravedigger runs to the room to find Ali dead in a pool of blood. The gravedigger holds his dead body and howls.

Haider notices the two soldiers coming closer. He quickly reaches an AK47 but fumbles as he tries to load it. The Ikhwaanis are barely a few feet away from him now, only a wall separates them. He struggles, barely managing to cock the weapon and fire rather amateurishly, killing one of the two just as they appear from behind the wall. The other retreats.

The grieving gravedigger picks up a grenade, runs out of the house and hurls it onto an Ikhwaan jeep. The jeep explodes, Khurram rolls over behind the rock as the bodies fly apart. The gravedigger is showered with bullets by the other Ikhwaanis.

196 EXT. ISLAMIC GRAVEYARD

Khurram gets up and looks from behind the rock. A few Ikhwaanis try to move towards the structure, Mohsin and Haider both fire bullets from different vantage points inside the house. They rush to different windows to fire more rounds, giving the impression of several people inside the house.

Ikhwaanis immediately turn back. Khurram pulls out his satellite phone and dials a number.

197 INT. ARMY CAMP - DAY

Murthy is in conversation with some officers inside his room. A junior officer walks in with a phone.

JUNIOR OFFICER

Sir, MLA Khurram Meer on the line.

MURTHY

Why?

JUNIOR OFFICER

Some Ikhwaan operation in outskirts. Asking for reinforcements.

Murthy remains poker-faced and silent. He turns back to his colleagues.

MURTHY

So you were saying that RR has supremacy over us? Rubbish.

The junior officer turns back and leaves.

CUT TO:

198 EXT. ISLAMIC GRAVEYARD

Khurram bangs his phone on the rock and looks at the Ikhwaan commander in frustration. They turn to the sound of a vehicle arriving from far.

A jeep with a few Ikhwaanis stops a few metres away. The soldiers show a rocket launcher from inside. A smile emerges in Khurram's eyes.

199 EXT. ISLAMIC GRAVEYARD

The Ikhwaani commander supervises the fixing of the rocket launcher from behind a rock.

200 EXT. ISLAMIC GRAVEYARD - OUTSKIRTS

Nearby, Roohdaar drives up in a jeep with Ghazala seated

next to him. They can hear the gun battle up ahead. They turn to each other, a beat.

He smiles and nods. She looks away, towards the battlefield.

CUT TO:

201 EXT. ISLAMIC GRAVEYARD

Khurram anxiously watches as an Ikhwaani soldier is ready to fire the rocket. The commander looks at Khurram, Khurram nods. The rocket is fired and hits the house. A huge explosion happens.

202 INT. ISLAMIC GRAVEYARD

The house rocks from inside as dust and smoke engulf the interior. Haider holds Arshia's body tightly in his arms and coughs as the debris falls over him. As the dust settles he notices Mohsin's dead body.

203 EXT. ISLAMIC GRAVEYARD

Another rocket is fixed to the launcher. The Ikhwaani soldier takes the aim to shoot but stops seeing his fellow soldier comes running towards them. The soldier stops near Khurram and shows him the walkie-talkie.

SOLDIER

आपकी बीवी...

Your wife, sir...

Khurram is amazed.

CUT TO:

204 EXT. ISLAMIC GRAVEYARD

A soldier escorts Ghazala to Khurram.

KHURRAM

आप क्या कर रहीं हैं यहाँ?

What are you doing here?

GHAZALA

(teary-eyed)

मेरे बेटे की जान बक़्श दो.

Please spare my son.

KHURRAM

आप समझ रही हैं... कि आप क्या कह रहीं हैं?

Do you realize what you're asking me to do?

Ghazala drops on her knees.

GHAZALA

एक मौका दे दो मुझे... वो मेरी बात नहीं टाल सकता...
सरेंडर कर देगा...

I'll get him to surrender... If you truly love me, give me one chance...

She looks at him with pleading eyes, Khurram looks on.

205 INT. ISLAMIC GRAVEYARD - DIGGER'S HOME

Arshia still in Haider's arms. Ghazala's voice echoes on the soundtrack.

GHAZALA

(off-screen on megaphone)

जाना....

My angel!

Haider reacts, he slowly gets up and climbs to the window to see Ghazala standing near one of the jeeps holding the megaphone. They look at each other from afar.

206 EXT. ISLAMIC GRAVEYARD

A temporary ceasefire of sorts. Khurram and the Ikhwaans keep a close watch as Ghazala walks towards the structure.

CUT TO:

207 INT. ISLAMIC GRAVEYARD-DIGGER'S HOME

Ghazala walks in. Dead bodies of the young Akram and the old gravedigger lie on the floor.

Haider makes his way down from the staircase, the AK47 slung across his shoulder. Ghazala looks at him, his face and clothes covered in blood. Ghazala breaks down seeing his condition.

GHAZALA

बचपन में तुझे खरोंच भी लग जाती थी तो
मैं सारा गाँव सर पे उठा लेती थी.

When you were a child I'd tear apart the
the world... if you got as much as a scratch...

She holds his face in between her palms.

GHAZALA

तू खूँ में नहाया है, और मैं चुपचाप देख रही हूँ.

You are covered in blood... and I can't do a thing.

She hugs him and cries.

HAIDER

मौजे... मैं सरेंडर नहीं करूँगा.

Mother... I won't surrender.

Ghazala smiles through her tears. She unties her head scarf and begins to drop it at his feet. Haider holds her hand and puts the scarf back on her head.

HAIDER

इस बार नहीं, मौजे.

Not this time.

GHAZALA

मुझे दोबारा बेवा नहीं देखना?

Don't you want to see me as a widow again?

Haider looks away.

GHAZALA

जाना...

Angel...

She holds his hand and whispers.

GHAZALA

अपनी औलाद का जनाज़ा देखने से बड़ा कोई दर्द नहीं है दुनिया में.

There's no greater pain... than to see the corpse of your child.

HAIDER

है.... अपने बाप का इंतक़ाम लिए बिना मर जाना.

There is... To die without avenging the murder of one's father.

Ghazala smiles sadly.

GHAZALA

इंतक़ाम से सिर्फ़ इंतक़ाम पैदा होता है. जब तक हम अपने इंतक़ाम से आज़ाद नहीं होंगे, तब तक कोई आज़ादी हमें आज़ाद नहीं कर सकती.

Revenge does not set us free… Freedom lies beyond revenge… True freedom…

Haider turns around to leave.

GHAZALA

आखिरी बार पूछ रही हूँ… सरेंडर कर दे वर्ना…

I beg you… drop your weapons, surrender... or else...

He stops, his back faces Ghazala.

HAIDER

वर्ना? मर जाएंगी आप?

Or else? You'll kill yourself?

A beat. She turns him around. They look at each other in silence. She kisses him on his forehead, eyes and finally gives a soft peck on his bloodied lips.

CUT TO:

208 EXT. ISLAMIC GRAVEYARD

Waiting outside, Khurram is on edge. Finally Ghazala walks out, their eyes meet. A beat. She walks towards Khurram, and the Ikhwaan soldiers.

Haider watches through the slit of a window. She is closer to Khurram and his army. She stops, her eyes are blank. She looks at Khurram, their eyes are locked. She slowly removes her shawl. The colour of Khurram's eyes changes. She wears a vest full of explosives joined through multiple wires. A small switch attached to the vest, hangs near her fingers.

Haider screams from inside the house.

HAIDER

मौजे!!

Mother!

Khurram's eyes dart towards the house. Haider comes out and runs to her. Khurram turns back to run.

Suddenly. BOOM!! She explodes!

Bodies of Ikhwaan soldiers fly in the air. Others are injured badly, there is chaos everywhere.

Through the fire and smoke emerges Haider - crying profusely.

HAIDER

मौजे!!

Mother!

As the dust and smoke settle we see a blood-soaked Khurram dragging himself along the ground, both his legs blown off.

Haider's eyes meet Khurram's. Crying, he takes out the pistol and heads towards the mutilated Khurram. Grabbing him by his hair, Haider pulls him up, places the gun on his eyes.

Blood oozes out of Khurram's severed legs, he screams as Haider tightens his grip. A beat. His mother's message resonates in his mind.

GHAZALA (voice-over)

इंतक़ाम से सिर्फ़ इंतक़ाम पैदा होता है. जब तक हम अपने इंतक़ाम से आज़ाद नहीं होंगे, तब तक कोई आज़ादी हमें आज़ाद नहीं कर सकती.

Revenge does not set us free... Freedom lies beyond revenge... True freedom...

He suddenly lets go of Khurram. Khurram can't make sense of what just happened as Haider limps away slowly, leaving him in a pool of blood.

KHURRAM

हैदर! मार दे मुझे... अपना इंतक़ाम पूरा कर... मार दे मुझे... मार दे...

Haider! I want to die... Avenge yourself... Kill me...

Haider slowly walks away into the smoke, leaving Khurram screaming for mercy. (Option 1- After a few steps he falls on the ground. Option 2- Roohdaar emerges from smoke. Smiling he opens his arms, Haider falls into his embrace.)

Top shot of the scene of the carnage. A gory painting of the bloodbath.

FADE TO BLACK.

END CREDITS ROLL